Send in the Wolf

THE GOOD GUYS' MR. WOLF

Jim Toner

VISION QUEST MEDIA
SCOTTSDALE, ARIZONA

Jim Toner/Vision Quest Media
27109 N. 143 Pl.
Scottsdale, AZ 85262
www.CreatingWealth101.com

Book Layout ©2013 BookDesignTemplates.com

Ordering Information:
Quantity sales. Special discounts are available on quantity purchases by corporations, associations, and others. For details, contact the "Special Sales Department" at the address above.

Send in the Wolf/ Jim Toner —1st ed.
ISBN 978-0-9912520-0-8

Contents

Dedication

To my wife, Allison, who has lived the crazy stories in this book with me.

My daughters, Justine and Natalie, who make me want to continue those crazy stories. You girls rock. I love you.

A special shout out to ALL of the entrepreneurs out there who fight the battle that keeps America great.
This country was and **is** *built on your backs, gang.*

Thanks!

Acknowledgments

The list of people who have come into our lives and given assistance can get pretty big. I, like most, owe a big thank you to lots of folks. So, I would like to extend another thank you to anyone from the past who has helped me as I learned the lessons in this book. Thanks again!

My biggest thank you goes to my wife Allison, and my daughters, Justine and Natalie. You see, I am crazy, and I have myself convinced that I have it hidden from them. I haven't. They just smile and put up with it. That's my girls! I love you.

A big thanks to the folks who were kind enough to lend their expertise in order to make this book a very valuable work. Roger and Sandy at Beverly International, Michael Roberts of Rexxfield, Kathy Svilar of KMS advertising, Missy Wilson of Be Real Management and Rich Selby of Selby Marketing. Awesome people that I recommend you do business with.

My friends and mentors Frank McKinney and Bill Bartmann . . . WOW, what can you say about having guys like that in your corner? Thanks for the advice and friendship.

What's an entrepreneur without other crazy entrepreneurs to bounce ideas off of? Thanks to Doug Doebler, Mark Evans, Phil Hardy, and Andrew Waite. My good guy attorneys Matt Nichols and Cris Ingle . . . you are a credit to your profession guys.

My team: Vince Parrucci, Rebecca Hall, Mary Malie, and John Fergeson . . . you guys rock!

A very special thanks to Kathleen Birmingham for helping me get this book together and correct my somewhat blunt approach.
LOL!
Thanks Kathleen.

While writing comes easy to me, it is still very important to be in a creative environment. I want to send a big thanks the world's best bar, Greasewood Flat and the world's best coffee shop, Janey's, in Cave Creek Arizona. Lots of inspiration from both places. Writing can be fun people; you just need to do it in the right place for you.

And last but not least, thanks to all the business owners and entrepreneurs out there that fight the good fight every day. You are the back bone of the country and I hope this book serves you well.

Foreword

Small business is the lifeblood of the American economy. The entrepreneurs of the last 200 years forged a path that led America to the Super Power status it still holds today.

Yes, business is serious business. Very serious. I know a bit of what I speak of as I myself came from very humble beginnings. As a teenager I was homeless and eating out of a dumpster. I was an alcoholic and paraplegic at eighteen after falling down a set of stairs drunk. Yet, I walked out of that hospital and I set my sights on something bigger than homelessness and gang activity.

I put myself through College, started a small business, and then the following...

- Voted National Entrepreneur of the year

- Nominated for the Nobel Peace Prize

- Borrowed 3.1 Billion dollars from 120 different lenders for privately held startup companies

- Named one of the top 100 entrepreneurs of that last 100 years

- Made the Forbes 400 list

- And, I became a Billionaire...then lost is all, in 72 hrs. And now, I am well on my way to getting it back.

So you see, I do know business, very, very well.

My friend, Jim Toner, has written a book that could prove priceless for you and your business. The gap between businesses using academia approaches and a real-world, proven, hard-earned approach is monumental.

Jim falls into the "been there, done that, got the T-shirt" category. He, just as I have, has been down, up, down, and back up again. I can assure you that the lessons learned on that journey are extremely valuable.

As you can see from Jim's bio, he is more than a proven commodity and does not rest on past accomplishments. In this book, you will find not only great strategies, but also brutal honesty. I have found that all too often in business people do not want to face the realities of the situation at hand. With Jim, you will have no choice. He is blunt, to the point and at times, irreverent. But most importantly, he speaks the truth.

Read this book. Soak it all in and take it to heart. You have a very valuable asset in your hands.

~Bill Bartmann
BillBartmann.com

I'm Winston Wolf...I solve problems.

—Pulp Fiction, 1994

I love that quote. For those of you who have not seen the movie, Winston Wolf is someone who is called in to clean up a BIG mess. He is the problem solver of *all* problem solvers.

For those of you who have seen it....well, no explanation needed.

My name is Jim Toner, but you can call me . . .

The Wolf . . .

I solve problems.

Business problems.

You may feel that you don't have any, but I beg to differ.

You *do* have problems. Some you may be ignoring. Some you may not see coming. And some that you know are there, but have no idea what to do about them.

That is where I come in. More on that later.

If you are currently a business owner or someone who is thinking about becoming a business owner, this book is for you. I will go so far as to say, *you NEED this book.*

Why Write This Book?

So, what are my reasons for writing this book? Why would I have an interest in helping business owners? I have my own business to deal with, right?

Let me tell you that one of the major reasons for this book is due to my belief in entrepreneurship and small business. Those two things are the backbone of this country. Without those, we are doomed. I don't like the idea of being doomed.

I want you to read this book as if I am talking specifically to you, like we're sitting down having a beer together. This is straight talk to a friend.

I have been an entrepreneur for almost thirty years, and a professional real estate investor for just about twenty-five of those years. I have, as they say, "seen it all." What I see now is causing me a great deal of concern...concern because it is contributing to the destruction of many small business owners and entrepreneurs.

Accurate Thinking

What's causing my concern?

The lack of accurate thinking!

Society has become so inundated with FAKE...that it alters people's perceptions. From the internet to social media to the real media . . . and I use that term loosely, we are pushed further and further away from the true reality of what it takes to become successful.

As a business owner/entrepreneur, you cannot afford to get caught in this trap. You need to be very aware of where you are at any given time in your business.

This book is about **REALITY . . .**

In my opinion, there is nothing that takes the place of entrepreneurship and being your own boss.

Nothing!

The ability to have total control over every aspect of your life is a very, very nice perk. But the perks are just the byproducts of running a successful business.

The key word here is *Successful.*

This book is about what it takes to get there.

Yes, being a business owner is one of the greatest, most gratifying ventures you will ever undertake. But the *reality* is that there will not just be obstacles along the way, but roadblocks and pipe bombs too.

There will be *lots* of them.

You must learn how to successfully deal with and/or negate their impact on you and your bottom line.

After reading halfway through this book you might feel that you have mistakenly picked up a horror novel because some of what you read will, and should, scare you. That however, can be a good thing. It will either wake you up to correcting an existing problem, or help you prevent an oncoming one.

These problems, many of which you don't even know to expect, are far reaching: from employees, to marketing, to cash flow, to partners, to attorneys, and CPAs, to government interference, vendors, competitors, etc. The list goes on and on.

Oh, by the way, you'll love the part about government interference.
(Just don't read it in the dark all alone.)

My point is this. It is called "business" for a reason. There are certain realities that you must confront in order to have a successful career as a business owner.

I know what I am talking about.

I have built multiple million dollar-plus businesses. As a result, I've been through:

- Employee issues
- Partner issues
- Government issues
- Cash flow issues
- Super highs and super lows

I have also seen very successful businesses destroyed overnight by refusing to acknowledge some of the topics in this book.

Yes, there are very real issues that you will encounter. And when you do, you need to know how to react. There is no shortage of namby-pamby advice available to you from management books with authors who have lots of letters after their name, as if this is some sort of reliable set of keys to the kingdom.

I am not knocking all the advice out there.

Admittedly, many of these people are far more book smart than I will ever be. But we are not talking about being book smart, are we? We are talking about *your* bottom line, and theory just doesn't cut it.

You will find no new age philosophy in this book.

What you will find is truth.

I know what I am talking about. I have friends and mentors who are mega-millionaires and even one who is a billionaire.

I have seen unprecedented success along with unimaginable failure. I have seen the "most likely to fail," succeed and "the most likely to succeed," fail.

I have gone from nothing more than a high school graduate to appearing on CNN, FOX, ABC, NBC, CBS, business journals, and national radio programs. I have taught thousands across the country how to create financial freedom through real estate investment as well as working with struggling business owners and getting them on the track towards profits and peace of mind.

I have been, and I am still, in the trenches. I not only live it, I am passionate about it! There is nothing that makes me happier that someone with the guts to step out on their own and go for it!

They grab life by the throat and scream,

GIVE ME WHAT I WANT!!!

This is what has made America great . . . people like you who have ventured into the unknown in hopes of creating a better life for yourself and your family.

And it is because of my passion for people like you, that I feel very protective.

I see on a daily basis how hard working business owners are being taken advantage of and I want to help...I CAN help. I speak from hard-earned experience and I have the scars to prove it.

My goal is to arm you to the teeth with hard-earned wisdom, resources, and inspiration needed in order to succeed AND make TONS of money, on your terms. You see, you will pay a price for your success. Win or lose, everybody pays, so let's make your price seem like the deal of the century.

So if you're ready to take this ride, all I ask of you is to LISTEN to me. Do not be so foolish as to think you can figure this out on your own. Learn from others mistakes as all successful people do. Should you choose to ignore my advice, well . . .

You'll see what happens then . . .

Note to Newbies

I am writing this book as if you are already in the game. That being said, some of you may be contemplating getting into the game so I want to make sure you are aware of what you are getting into.

Let's get right to the point here. There is no half way. When you have made the decision to be a business owner, or continue to be a business owner/entrepreneur, you must adhere to the advice of Yoda:

"Do, or do not. There is no try."

That funny looking but very wise little guy is right.

There is no try.

It's sometimes hard to explain, this "entrepreneur" thing. I guess the best way to describe it is a "knowing", that you are different. A knowing that there is something better out there for you. A knowing that you are not like everyone else, and you will not settle for what it is everyone else settles for.

You just know.

Warning #1

Now here is the first of my many warnings you will find throughout this book. If you DON'T know if this is the life for you and are just "kicking around the idea" or you want to dabble in a business enterprise to just "see how it works out," let me save you lots of time, money and heartache.

DON'T DO IT!

It's not for you. As I said, there is no half way. You don't dip your toes in the water. You jump in off the deep end.

One of the primary reasons for becoming an entrepreneur or business owner is MONEY. Let's be honest . . . it IS about the money.

Lots of money.

When you are talking about making lots of money, you also have to include the price for attaining said riches. No, it does not come free. As a matter of fact, the price is high . . . sometimes too high for many to pay.

If you are not willing to go all out, all day, every day, this is not the path for you. This is a game of daily battles that must be fought and won in order to continue. And if you're not up for daily battles, you're not up for it at all.

Period.

The great Les Brown has a perfect quote:

> *Life is a daily battle for territory.*
> *Once you stop fighting for what you want,*
> *what you **don't** want, automatically takes its place.*

Think on that one for a bit. "A ***daily*** battle for territory." You need to answer this question for yourself. Are you willing to fight this battle? Are you willing to get kicked in the teeth and beaten down only to get back up again and say . . . bring it on?

Are you?

Now this is one of those, "Come to Jesus moments," where you need to be VERY honest with yourself. Can you take the hit? If you are already an entrepreneur, can you continue to take the hits?

They keep coming you know. They come from all directions.

They come from friends, family members, co-workers, media, government and even other so-called entrepreneurs. The biggest enemy you will face however . . . is YOU!

Yes, you.

That ever-present voice in your head that says you:

- Are not qualified
- Are not smart enough
- Don't have enough money
- Don't have enough skills
- Don't have enough connections, experience, etc., etc., etc.

This is why Les Brown said what he did. A *daily* battle for territory.

I can now see heads nodding in agreement as well as people putting down the book saying entrepreneurship is not for them.

It is what it is.

So for those of you who are still reading, great, you're in for some tough lessons, but they'll make you far more successful. Let's assume that you do want this life and you are willing to take the hit, or are willing to continue taking the hits. You're now asking, "How do I fight these battles?"

All battles must have a battle plan and in all battles you must know your enemy. And once the enemy has been identified, you can fight.

As I mentioned, the biggest and most constant battle will be fought with yourself. It comes in the form of the voice in your head that creeps in from time to time and tells you to throw in the towel. It whispers, "This battle will never end."

No matter how successful you become, at some point, doubt will creep in, which is why you must always be sharpening your sword.

Remember This:

If you worry about what others think, you will fail.
If you think you're not good enough, you will fail.
If you cannot convince yourself you ARE good enough, you will fail.
If you are afraid of failure, you will fail.
Permanently.
If you are not prepared to do what others will not, you will fail.

Here is a little tip ...

When that voice creeps into your head
and starts whispering to you in a negative way,
scream at the top of your lungs ...
SHUT UP!!!!

Yeah, that's right.
Tell yourself to shut up.
That may sound silly, but it works.

Good News

Listen, there is good news. If you think that the accumulation of money has anything to do with anything other than a decision, then put this book back on the shelf now. You will not make it, because the truth is . . .

Money does not care who gets it!

Money does not discriminate. Money does not care if you are black or white or short or fat or ugly or handsome. Money goes to those who attract it through their thoughts and actions. Money is neutral and will go to those who decide to get it.

That was a big clue there.

Money goes to those who decide . . . not hope for or think about . . . **DECIDE.**

Success is nothing more than a decision. You cut off all possibilities other that the path that leads to your goal. Ok, that was the good news. If you're ugly you still got a shot.

Enemy number one, which is you, has been identified.

Bad News

Who's next?

Look around, the enemy is everywhere. If I had to start somewhere it would be with the legion of "well meaning" people in your life who are more than willing to give you a daily beat down.

I call these people the "walking dead."

No affiliation to the TV show, but by the looks of some of them, you would never know. They have that grey, dead look about them; that look, by the way, comes from working a job you hate, for an unsatisfactory paycheck, and enough stress to choke a horse. They hate their life, and they know it. They are addicted to steady paychecks and perceived security like a junkie to crack.

They do, however, want to tell you how foolish you are to consider such a venture, or to continue chasing a stupid dream. They try to persuade you with their impassioned questions, "Wouldn't you rather have the security of a real job with two weeks paid vacation?"

Yeah, and for that real job security, you have to sit in traffic every day, go to a job you don't like, but hey, you should do it because it's what everybody does.

That says it all right there.

They want you to be like them. They want you to stay in their group. I mean really, if you get out and make it, what will that say of them? They want you to fail . . . for them. It is their hang-up they're afraid of, and they're putting that burden, that expectation on you.

They will tell you all the horror stories of failed businesses.
They will tell you how bad the economy is.
They will tell you there is too much competition and that you can't do it.

They want your soul. They want you to throw in the towel on your dream just as they did. They want you to be weak.

Adding insult to injury, the media hits you with a constant barrage of negativity and class warfare. They have TV shows devoted to the rich and famous. Something that you will never be is the underlying message. As a consolation prize however, you can watch someone else live his or her dreams on TV.

And if it's on TV, it's gotta be real, right?

The lists of those people or mediums who are looking to keep you down are endless.

To combat this, you must have a strong belief in yourself and your goal. You need to be persistent. Not bull-headed, not unwilling to adjust course.

Persistent.

You need to trust your gut instincts. This is an invaluable tool that is too often ignored. Do not ignore it. You have gut instinct for a reason.

You need to continually learn and adjust. The minute you think you've "made it" and you stop doing what brought you to the dance, you will find yourself in a death spiral. Do not ignore my warning on this one. Never *ever*, stop working on yourself and getting better.

Life Isn't Fair

Above all else you need to remember that life is not fair. No one ever said it was. No one ever said it would be easy. Everybody pays. Rich, poor, young, old. Everybody. As an entrepreneur sometimes it seems that you may be paying more than your fair share. I get it, I've been there, but that's the game, and it's what you signed up for.

You need to keep your prospective when you're getting piled on.

Ask the kid in Haiti who hasn't eaten in a week about fairness. Ask the mother who just lost a child about fairness. Ask a promising young athlete who just became a quadriplegic about fairness. No, life is not fair, and neither is business.

It can be cold, cutthroat, and dirty.

But the payoff should you succeed? Not just the money. Your life, your soul, the power to control every part of your life.

This power to run your life the way you see fit is the real payoff.

You run the show. Yeah, you take the hits, but you also get the glory. You get the "knowing" that you weren't just one of the mindless masses being controlled to do the bidding of others.

I can assure you that there is great satisfaction in standing tall, bloody but unbowed. Knowing that you understood that we get one shot on this earth and you had the guts to take it. To be honest, sometimes that is even better than the money.

But we'll still take the money.

We always take the money.

So now that you are primed and ready to go, I am going to break this down into what I feel are the most important things you need to know in order to succeed.

NONE OF THIS IS THEORY

You may not like much of what I have to say. You may even ignore what I have to say. I will caution you against this approach. Don't fall into the trap of thinking, "My business is different, so it doesn't apply."

No, it's not.

We are all in the same business and you are not immune to what lurks in the shadows.

By reading all the way through this book, you will receive some very valuable insights on how to not only protect yourself, but how to **POSITION** yourself in the market place.

You may also be very surprised how obvious some of this advice is. My question, then, to you is:

"If it is so bleeping obvious, why are you not following it?"

It is not good enough just to "know" something.

You need to implement.

Everything in this book requires implementation. If that sounds like a lot of work, look at it this way: everything you implement will either *save*, or *make* you lots of money.

Oh, by the way, I've included some incredibly valuable bonus material in this book.

Because I know my way around the business world, I have identified and interviewed a few leaders in the industry in the fields of:

- **Customer Service**

- **Marketing**

- **Reputation Management**

If you read nothing else, ***read these interviews***.

They will save you time, headaches, and above all else, money.

CHAPTER 1

It's All On You, Baby

I decided **not** to save the best for last. Instead, I think it warrants being put first. This is not a strategy, per se. It is **the** ingredient to success. Yes, there really is one, and this is it:

> *Work harder on yourself than you do at your job.*
>
> —JIM ROHN

Despite his death, Jim Rohn not only continues to be one of my mentors, but he was a mentor to hundreds of thousands, if not millions, of entrepreneurs throughout the world. His best known student is Tony Robbins, the world-famous self-help guru.

Jim Rohn said that the problem with most people is they continue wishing for some*thing* to get better and hoping that will change his or her circumstances.

Many people are looking to change some*thing*, but that is not how it works. What needs to change is you. That's when everything else gets better.

When I first heard Jim Rohn's words all those years ago, it took a while for them to sink in. I really think it was so obvious that I missed it. I was a young entrepreneur, doing what I thought was my best but I was still struggling.

I kept wishing for things to change . . . on the outside.

I hoped for the real estate market to change. I hoped the people I was surrounding myself with would change. I was looking for everything to change, except me.

I believe it was Gandhi who said, "Be the change you wish to see in the world."

I probably heard *that* before too, but I never applied to me.

Eventually, it sunk in.

And it really didn't take that long. What a simple, but powerful statement. "Work harder on yourself than you do at your job."

This is the secret:

If *I* get better, then **everything** gets better.

I was not necessarily sure it was going to work, but I had nothing to lose. So I went to work...on ME. I became an information junkie. I bought every book I could find on business, real estate investment, marketing, and so on.

Education and Personal Development

I enrolled in what Zig Ziglar called the "automobile university."

I did not get into my car without a personal development tape program ready to play as I drove. I listened to thousands of hours of motivational and business programs.

I received a world-class education in my car.

I bought biographies on all the great leaders. I learned from THEM what to do and what not to do.

Here is a news flash for you:

Any problem you may have in life and business has been experienced by someone else before you. You can find out how they solved that problem! That, to me, was unbelievable. Like most entrepreneurs, I thought I was on an island all alone.

No!

It's all been done before, and the answers are just waiting for you to pick them up.

I also took the advice of one of my other truly great mentors, Charlie "TREMENDOUS" Jones, who said:

You will be the same person five years from now as you are today except for the books you read and the people you meet.

Who Do You Spend Time With?

I had the book and audio thing down, but I was still lacking on the "people you meet" part.

What that means is, "Who are you hanging around with?" This can be a killer for you and your business unless you deal with it *now.*

When I started my career as a real estate investor, I surrounded myself with people that were, to be kind, not up to par. On a personal level, all my friends were broke and complaining about everyone and everything which, unbeknownst to me, had a very bad effect on my attitude.

No one in my inner circle took personal responsibility.

Looking back, that's why I was stuck for so long.

When I read deeper into Charlie's quote, I realized that he didn't just mean people, he meant better people. Yes, in my business life, I had people who were so-called "experts" in their field. Realtors, contractors, finance people, etc., but they were not *really* experts, they were just in the business.

I began to seek out the **BEST** that I could find.

Once I did this, I noticed a rapid and dramatic jump in my income. Next, I began to withdraw from many of my friends of the time. I was growing and they were not. They needed to go. This may be difficult for you, but here is the reality.

Not everybody makes it.

Some need to be left behind.

This may sound harsh, but that is the way it is. If you have an inner circle that does not *completely* support you and are striving for the best in their own lives, you need distance yourself from them.

This was not an overnight process. There were still bumps in the road, but as each day passed, I grew better equipped to handle the realities of entrepreneurship.

My priority and your priority, was and *must* be **WORKING ON YOU**.

This is not an option.

You *must* make your main focal point YOU!

- **YOU getting better**

- **YOU getting around better people**

- **YOU getting better information**

These are the keys to the kingdom.

This is why great franchises can be so good for some. They provide all the ammunition you need to become successful. Information. Product. Team. Backup.

Everything.

You can walk into any McDonalds, anywhere in the world, and an eighteen-year-old kid can be running the show. Why? Well it's not because they have the market cornered on smart eighteen-year-old kids. It's because they have made it fool-proof by providing the necessary information, tools, and people.

This simple concept changed my entire life.

If you look at my bio it looks pretty impressive. What makes it even more impressive is that I barely made it out of high school! I was *not* a book smart individual. I would have never made it if it had not been for that piece of advice. I can say with full confidence, that advice creates miracles.

Brain vs. Brawn

There is more to it than just feeding your head. You need to take care of the body. Oh, I can hear the groans now. Pay close attention to me on this. The mind and the body go together.

If one is lacking, all is lacking.

You cannot operate a business at its highest level if you are not physically fit. I'm not talking about being a body builder or world-class athlete, but fit. And fit as you can get for your age unless you have some *serious* health issues that would prevent that.

I have worked out my entire life and I am in better shape than many who are half my age. Just a fact. I work at it. Do I like going to the gym? No, I hate it!

I do, however, like the results.

And the results also register in financial form. The biggest crisis this country is facing is not the economy, but health care. Almost 50% of Americans are considered obese.

Have you ever heard the term, "survival of the fittest"? Well, it's true. Not only will you last longer than the competition, you will attract more business.

You must make yourself attractive to the marketplace in all areas. Product, service, and appearance. Deny it all you want, but people gravitate to attractive people. I didn't say it's fair, but it is what it is.

Refer to my opinion on "fair."

To win in today's business climate, today's **very competitive** climate, you must be on your game at all levels. You have no choice but to take an active role in being as physically fit as possible. And yes, you have the time. You need 30-45 minutes a day of vigorous exercise, along with a sensible eating plan to keep yourself at the top of your game. I suggest a regimen of weight training, assuming you have no physical ailments, along with twenty minutes of daily cardio. And I don't mean walking at a snail's pace on a treadmill. I mean *vigorous,* "break a sweat, work your body" effort.

You have been given the greatest machine ever created. Care for it. If you do, you will be rewarded. If you don't, you will pay the price. If you need help, hire a personal trainer.

And what about that eating plan I mentioned? Sooooo much misinformation out there, where do you start? You're in luck. I happen to have forgotten more about nutrition than most so-called experts know.

Hey, it ain't bragging if it's true.

Almost 70% of your fitness level and physical appearance will be derived from the eating plan and 30% from working out. Most people think the opposite. They think they can eat as much as they want as long as they work out. Unless you're burning 5,000 calories a day, you need to watch what type and how much fuel goes into the machine. And even if you are burning big calories, you still need the right fuel.

Here is the easiest and best plan you will ever find. If it doesn't walk, fly, swim or grow out of the ground, don't eat it.

I just saved you all the trouble of going out and wasting money on useless diet books and programs. The above-mentioned plan is how we are genetically programmed.

All this nonsense with processed foods, bread, sugars, was not meant for us and I think the result is pretty obvious. To compound the problem, we not only eat the wrong things, we **overeat** the wrong things. Add that to the stress of being a business owner **and** not exercising, you can see how disaster could be fast approaching.

If you really want to take a serious interest in your health, which you must, check out www.bevnut.com. This is the website of Beverly Nutrition. You will see my interview with the owners in the Customer Service chapter. The fitness info they give away on their site is a literal gold mine.

Booze

And last but not least . . . it's got to be five o'clock somewhere. Look, this is the tough one for lots of people.

The booze.

I get it.

The life of an entrepreneur, for all its great rewards, does come with stress. Lots of it. I also know that sometimes a good shot of whiskey can go a long way. I know that some time at the bar after a hard day can provide a measure of relief.

I also know that sometimes . . . the party never ends.

I have been blessed with some type of freak genetics or maybe Irish blood that allowed me to drink . . . a *lot* and still be productive.

Or so I thought.

It was only after I stopped drinking, that I realized how unproductive I was. Yes, I was functioning, but when I look back on what I could have done had I not been drinking, it's pretty sad. Not to mention the fact that excessive drinking will ruin any fitness plan you may have.

I am not, nor have I ever have been, an alcoholic.

I am one of those people who can say, that's it, I'm done. I still enjoy an occasional drink now and then, but for the most part I have seriously backed off.

If you can, I suggest you consider doing the same. It's not the end of the world. You may shock yourself at how productive and less stressed you become. If you can't quit . . . get some help. There is no shame in asking for help in this matter. We all have demons that we need to keep locked away. And I mean we **ALL** have them. Even the ultra-wealthy and super-successful.

Deep down, we are all the same. No one better, no one worse. If this is your demon, keep it in the cage. I promise that having a clear head will have a positive effect on more than just your bottom line.

The lesson in this chapter is exactly what we started with. Make YOU getting better a priority.

"Work harder on yourself, than you do at your job."

If you don't read, start.

Now!

If you do read . . . Continue and add to it.

Buy and listen to tape/CD/MP3 programs; personal development, business, marketing, and any other subject that will help you grow. I will provide you with a list of "must haves" at the end of the book.

Network and reach out to those who can help you get to the next level and eliminate, or at least distance yourself, from those who holding you down. Find people who are **better** than you at **everything!** You will be pleasantly surprised how the most successful people are always willing to help or pass on some good advice.

Take a serious interest in your health. And I mean serious. You must become attractive to the marketplace. Mentally, physically, and with your products and service.

When you follow this plan of self-improvement in your life, magic happens. You will wonder what happened as things that were once so difficult now come so easily. This is no smoke and mirrors, this **WORKS**. It is timeless wisdom that can turn your life and business around. I know. It did for me.

Momentum

And now the *warning*.

I also know what happens when you stop.

You see, I did everything that I have recommended to you. And guess what? I became a big success, I made **LOTS** of money. As a matter of fact . . . obscene amounts of money.

I was the big dog and I was too smart for my own good.

I thought I knew it all.

I was so smart I decided that I no longer needed to follow the principles that got me to the dance. I stopped reading, listening to audio programs, stopped working out or at least half-assed my way through my workouts, and it all . . . began . . . to crumble.

It took me almost a year-and-a-half to figure out what was happening. I was looking everywhere to point the blame except for where it belonged.

With me!

What snapped me out of it? Wouldn't you know it was the same thing that made me successful? I remembered a quote by my friend, the great Les Brown and here is what it said:

<u>WRITE THIS DOWN AND KEEP IT WITH YOU:</u>

Life is a constant battle for territory.

The minute you stop fighting for what you want,

What you don't want, automatically takes its place.

That was the answer I had been looking for.

I had stopped fighting.

I had stopped reaching.

I had stopped growing.

Thankfully, I was able to recognize what was happening and course correct. I assure you that I will never make that mistake again. I say, without hesitation, that I am now better in every way than I have ever been.

There is no tomorrow. Only today.

You need to focus on being the very best you can be and you need to do it *now*.

Either cut down or eliminate all forms of distraction in terms of outside messaging. This means the internet, social media, the news, and so on. This is nothing more than mass brainwashing and if you think it does not have an effect on you, you are dead wrong.

Focus _**only**_ on _**you**_ getting _**better**_.

If what you have around you or going into your head or your body is not adding, then it is subtracting.

Get rid of it.

When you get better, everything gets better.

Trust me.

You will get many valuable lessons from this book, but this is the one that I hope you take to heart. **_You_** are the most valuable asset you have.

Don't blow it.

CHAPTER 2

One is the Loneliest Number

W hen Three Dog Night recorded that song I wonder if they knew what great business advice it would be. One "anything" in business can put you in a position you do not want to be in.

Andrew Carnegie once said:

Put all your eggs in one basket, and watch that basket very closely.

Now far be it from me to question the wisdom of someone like Andrew Carnegie, but I'm going to. Rich, does not always mean right.

Why? Because, as they say, "Shit happens."

You get bored, things break, people leave, trends change and on and on.

When change occurs, which it always does, you need to have a fallback position. As a matter of fact, oftentimes you may find that the fallback position takes the place of the primary position.

So, the word of the day is...DIVERSIFY.

Just look for examples at Apple, Trump, Richard Branson, and many other very successful individuals. They branch out into as many things as they can, knowing that some of these ventures will fail. They don't go into it "knowing" it is going to fail, but they understand that in business, sometimes things just don't work out. They also are taking advantage of the leverage multiple income streams operated simultaneously can bring.

Listen, it is very important for you to understand who you really are. You are an entrepreneur. You are not a coffee shop owner or a landscaper or a fitness trainer, YOU ARE AN ENTREPRENEUR.

Entrepreneurs go where the money is. Get it? As some of my clients down south say, "Yer a money finder and getter." Yup, I am, and so are you.

So what you need to do in addition to working on and growing your primary gig is to actively begin to scout out more and more opportunities to make more baskets.

I can hear some of you now disagreeing with me by thinking that you "are" what you "do." No, you are not. Ray Crock was a milkshake maker salesman. How did he go from that to owning the biggest restaurant chain in the world? He knew he wasn't "just" a milkshake maker salesman.

He was an entrepreneur.

If you are not in a constant state of evolution, you are edging closer to a state of extinction.

So what kind of basket do you look for? Well, that depends, as there are more opportunities out there than you can count. I personally like investment real estate.

Let me make my case here. Some of you may be thinking I am promoting investment real estate because of my past and current history with it. I think that it is very important for you to understand however, that I got into the investment real estate biz, not because I liked houses. I got into it because I liked MONEY.

Many moons ago when I finally came to the realization that the "traditional" path to making money was not working, I set out to find something that would. Frankly, I didn't care what I did as long as it would supply me with the money I needed to live the lifestyle I was looking for.

So I went out to look for my basket. It didn't take me long to make a very important discovery...RICH PEOPLE HAD REAL ESTATE.

As a matter of fact it was Andrew Carnegie himself who said:

"MORE MILLIONAIRES HAVE BEEN CREATED THROUGH REAL ESTATE THAN ANY OTHER ENDEAVOR."

That was all I needed to hear. Remember, I didn't know anything about it, didn't really care about it, and I didn't have the necessary skills. None of that mattered.

I am not going to go into my entire back story in this chapter but what I will say is that within 45 days, I had made more money than I had made in working six months at my job. The best part is that it was passive income, meaning that I did not have to physically work for it.

Here are some of the reasons you can and should consider making investment real estate one of your baskets.

1. It is a tangible asset. Meaning you can see it, touch it. It's really there and not just your money floating out in the ether.

2. It is an active market. Unless everyone plans on moving out into the street, you will always have an active market and it will never go out of style.

3. OPM. In case you don't know what that is, it's Other People's Money. Yes, you really can get into this biz all by using someone else's money.

4. Passive Income. This is the big one. Investment real estate can run with minimal involvement from you. This gives you the huge advantage of spending your time doing the things you really want to do.

5. Low Risk. There is nothing you can get into that is a no risk venture and I mean nothing. Walking across the street has risk. The question is, "What degree of risk?" In the investment world, risk and reward ratio goes hand in hand. This means if you want to get a high return on an investment, you are looking at high risk. If you want maximum safety, you will be looking at a very low return. Real estate offers the opportunity for a very high return with

a very low risk. It is an entirely different animal in the investment world.

6. Opportunity for Profit. This was the big draw for me in the beginning. I wanted to make LOTS of money and make it fast. In this business, averaging $25,000 - $50,000 on a flip is not a freak occurrence, it is the norm. Add to that the fact that you are doing it with other people's money, time, and talent, and you have the greatest thing since sliced bread.

7. Flexibility. This is what makes it such a good basket. As I said earlier, this business can truly run with very little of your involvement. Whatever your primary baby is may require a significant amount of your time. By adding real estate, you add the potential for huge additional income with very little time involvement.

Those are the big seven. Obviously there are many more opportunities out there other than investment real estate, but I think it is one of the best, if not **the** best. Remember our golden rule. GO WHERE THE MONEY IS. And the money, lots of it, is in investment real estate.

So go out and build some more baskets.

Don't be fooled into thinking you are not in the extinction line. Many, many others much bigger than you have ignored this rule with disastrous results.

Just ask the record companies.

CHAPTER 3

Employees

N o cute title for this chapter.

"One word will suffice," he said as he wrote the word, teeth clenched.

I found this chapter difficult to write and it will probably be difficult for many of you to read:

- Many of you will not want to hear what I have to say because you are in denial.
- Many will read and nod in agreement with what I am saying and do nothing.
- Some of you, the smart ones, will underline, re-read, and *ACT* on what I am saying.

Your choice.

Before I go any further I will concede that there are exceptions to every rule. Obviously, there are great employees out there and some of them may be with you. I get that.

However, from a *sheer numbers* point of view, the odds are stacked against you. You are far more likely to have average or below average employees. As for thinking you have well above average and exceptional employees? Well, as the old saying goes, "Even a blind pig roots up an ear of corn every once and a while."

Sometimes you get lucky, but not too often.

In fact, very, *very* rarely.

Much of how the odds lay will be determined by how carefully you bring someone into your business. Hire employees with your *eyes wide open* so you are not blindsided. For those of you new to the employee thing . . . this will help you plan. For those of you already in the water, this will help you course-correct.

I do have a bit of experience in this subject as I have had as many as thirty employees and as few as one. The number of employees isn't what counts. It's how you manage them.

If you can't manage one, you can't manage thirty.

The reason I said this is difficult for me to write is because I don't have much to say about "it". Frankly, I could sum up the entire chapter in one paragraph. That however will probably not sink in as you may assume that the brevity equates to importance.

Nothing could be further from the truth.

As a matter of fact, I could fill an entire book on this subject. In my coaching programs, I do go into this subject in **MUCH** greater detail.

For the purpose of this book though, I am going to keep it brief, but not too brief.

Necessary Evil

These two words fit quite well.

Unfortunately, most people cannot go it alone in business without some type of help. There are some small businesses where you can pull it off and a number of franchises that lend themselves to this option. Outsourcing, too, minimizes the need for full-time employees for some types of business.

In my opinion, the fewer employees you need, the better. But sometimes you do need a few.

Let me begin with my philosophy on employees. Now, some of you liberal, touchy feely types may be offended by this so be warned.

THE ONE AND ONLY PURPOSE OF AN EMPLOYEE IS TO PUT MORE MONEY IN MY POCKET AND MAKE MY LIFE EASIER!

Sound harsh?

Hey, sometimes the truth hurts.

How did I arrive at this "philosophy"? I was born and raised in Homestead, Pennsylvania, a suburb ten miles outside of Pittsburgh.

My father worked in the steel mills his entire life and instilled in me what I feel to be a very strong work ethic. At one point, I even considered getting a job in the mills when I graduated high school. That is until my dad taught me a lesson I will never forget. As a matter of fact, I can remember his words like it was yesterday.

When I told him I wanted to follow in his footsteps, he said, "You need to find something else to do with your life. The mills will not be there by the time you graduate high school. You cannot pay someone $8.00 an hour to sleep all night. The union demands for more pay for less work will be the end of it all."

Well, he was right. The union demands did help put an end to the steel mills.

The mentality was that if the company made more money, the employees should make more money whether it was deserved or not. Not only did they feel that way, they abused the process. My dad told me about guys working the overnight shift who would **SLEEP** all night and then brag about it. $8.00 an hour was a lot of money back in 1979, especially when you're paying for someone to sleep.

My point is this. The entire country has been overwhelmed with an entitlement mentality of, "Give me more, give me more. I don't want to have to earn it, just give it to me. "

Fortunately, or unfortunately, this is how I view employees. My experiences only serve to emphasize my dad's observations. I've had a lot of employees over the years and without exception, I repeat, **without exception** at some point or another they all developed that entitlement mentality.

I can hear some of you saying, "Yeah Jim, I can see your point, but I have some very good people working for me." Well, I'm sure you do. I did too. Or at least I thought I did. I thought I had people who were *so* loyal they would be with me forever and follow me to hell and back.

Guess what, they didn't and they don't.

The basic instinct of the human being is survival.

Their survival, not yours.

If it comes down to you or them, trust me, they are not going to worry about you or your family.

It is absolutely critical for you to remember this.

If you are looking for loyalty, get a dog, not an employee.

THE ONE AND ONLY PURPOSE OF AN EMPLOYEE IS TO PUT MORE MONEY IN MY POCKET AND MAKE MY LIFE EASIER!

Yeah, I said it again.

On purpose.

Your reasons may be different, and they never cease to amaze me. If I listed all the stupid reasons people hire employees, this would be a very long chapter. But the above mantra should guide you.

If you appreciate the seriousness of my statement, let's move on to **who** fills the role you have available and **what** they will be doing for you.

Whether you need a single key person or you need fifty employees will depend on your business. In my experience, many business owners bring in more employees than necessary, others don't bring on enough.

The key to success is to know exactly how many people you need in order to obtain maximum productivity and maximum profits.

Hot Tip

Just because you need something done doesn't mean you have to hire employees. Many needs can be met by outsourcing. A restaurant can't outsource the cooks, servers, etc. But a small gift shop owner who needs a website doesn't need to hire a full-time web designer.

Make sense?

So, assuming that you **DO** need employees . . . how do we manage and deal with these kids?

First, you make it very, very clear why they are there and what is expected of them. This is the biggest reason employers have problems with their employees. It is super important to let them know up front, the philosophy of the company. You need to bring in someone who "gets it." Most, however, will hire someone who will bring more misery than anything else. Why?

You didn't explain the rules!

Compare this to real estate investment. The biggest reason landlords have trouble with tenants is because 99.9% of the time, they didn't explain the rules. When the rules aren't explained the tenant makes his own rules, i.e. not paying the rent, prostitution ring, drug dealing, etc.

Employees are no different.

They may not run drugs or be the local pimp, but they **will** play when the cat is away . . . You must clearly outline the duties and responsibilities of any and all employees. If you do not, why would you be surprised if they did not do what you want them to do?

I mean really? **WHY** would you be shocked?

Yet so many business owners want to point the finger at rotten employees when in fact, it is the business owner who is the problem. That's not to say the employee wasn't a bad choice initially, but to make an employee a good one is *your* responsibility.

The Plan

Outline very clear and detailed responsibilities that can be measured and managed. **Write** them down. If you can't measure it, you can't manage it. Your employees can't perform well when they don't know what is expected.

Once expectations are clear, you must manage the process, which doesn't mean hovering over their shoulder every minute. If you must do this, you hired the wrong person.

With this kind of structure you can track progress and measure results.

Here is a list of *my* deal-killers in terms of employees:

Tardiness

This to me, is a "do not pass go, you are done" card. I totally understand that there are times when being late cannot be helped. But, those times are very few and far between. Maybe I am a bit anal, but my philosophy is that if you are not fifteen minutes early, you are late. When people are consistently late, that shows a **BIG** lack of respect for **YOU**. In effect, their tardiness says that their time is much more important than yours.

Sorry. You're done!

I strongly recommend that you make this very clear to any potential employees, and that there is no quarter given. If you choose to let someone into your business with this habit and attitude, I absolutely guarantee that they will burn you at some point.

When you have a tardy employee, immediately sit down with them and get it handled. Even if you need them for whatever reason, let them know their tardiness will no longer be tolerated. No other explanations needed.

You own the business.

If this tardy employee is one you simply haven't got the guts to fire...then put on your big boy or big girl pants and **FIRE** them. Once you do, let everyone know *why* you fired them and that you will no longer tolerate lateness.

"But Jim, they might get mad at me."

Whaaa. Whaaa. Whaaa. Toughen up.

I am going to repeat this over and over and over until you get it.

This is *your* business.

This is *your* livelihood.

This is *your* paycheck.

Forget the touchy-feely crap and run your business like a business. If you want to do charity work, go to your local church.

Misuse of Time

When you are paying someone to perform a task that means they need to be performing the task. Silly me, expecting someone to do what I am paying them to do. But I **DO** expect someone to do what I am paying them to do.

I suggest you be silly too. I'd bet that you would be horrified if I installed some hidden cameras in your workplace and monitored what your employees are doing with **YOUR** time.

If I were to do that I could tell you they are surfing the web, making personal phone calls, chit chatting with other employees, sleeping, and any number of things that do not pertain to the job you hired them for.

And you're *paying* them to do these things.

So how do you deal with this? Well, the first way is to prevent it in the first place. Just as with being late, this needs to be dealt with up front or if you already have employees in place, immediately after you read this.

I recommend a zero tolerance policy in dealing with these issues. I know that sounds harsh and maybe it is. As a result of my past experience, when I was overly lenient on these issues, I found myself making excuses for them.

I didn't want to be the "bad boss" because I wanted everyone to like me.

Being the nice boss didn't work for me and it won't work for you.

Promises, Promises

I had employees that I swore up and down would never ever do anything to hurt me. I would bend over backwards for them and I was sure my kindness and loyalty would be rewarded.

It wasn't.

Of the two of the people I put at the top of that list, one embezzled a couple hundred thousand dollars from me and almost put me out of business and the other quit out of the blue and went to work for a competitor she had consistently bad-mouthed.

On another occasion, the real estate brokerage where I was co-owner hired a property manager that I had a funny feeling about. Nice guy, almost too nice . . . a real schmoozer. I had a bad vibe about him from the start. I couldn't put my finger on it, but I knew something wasn't right.

However, I was not in charge of this individual and my partner, who was the broker of record, assured me that it was my imagination.

One day, I was contacted by one of *my* clients asking me about potential deals that were being sent to them. I had no idea what he was talking about until I saw the e-mail.

This property manager was using **MY** database of customers to sell **HIS** real estate deals on the side!

As you can probably imagine, I was just a little bit ticked off.

My partner however, though it was an honest mistake and that he was a valuable employee. Honest mistake? Soliciting my database without my permission? No, not an honest mistake. Back-door theft is more like it.

I made the mistake of letting my partner talk me out of firing him and just letting him off with a warning.

The thing is where there is smoke there is fire and this kid would strike again.

Sure enough, not long after, we began receiving calls from clients asking about their rent payments. It seems they had not been receiving them. When my partner at the time *finally* agreed to confront him about this, the kid gave another song and dance.

Then he quit.

We found thousands of dollars in rent checks in his desk that had not been deposited. He had been spending his days **not** out at client properties but out looking for his own properties all the while being paid a salary by us.

He left quite a mess for us to clean up. The real fault, however, belonged to my partner and me.

I knew something was wrong. My gut told me from the start that something wasn't right. We should have taken a closer look at the guy in the beginning. We definitely should have fired the guy after the client solicitation incident.

I violated my own rule. I let my partner talk me out of listening to my gut.

Are You Listening to Your Gut?

I'd put up a significant wager that some of you reading this have employees right now who you have a bad "gut feeling" about.

And you're trying to convince yourself that "things will work out."

Please, that's no different than when you were a kid and you pulled the covers over your head telling yourself there is no monster.

When you were a kid, you were right.

This time, the monster is real and ignoring its presence is a *huge* mistake.

There is a reason the phrase "hire slow, fire fast," has been around for so long. You alone are responsible for your employee policy; what you will tolerate and what you will not tolerate.

My tolerance level is zero. Unless it is a really small issue, you don't get a second chance with me.

Hiring Employees

Let's back up for a minute and assume that you don't have any employees, and you have determined that you absolutely have the need.

How do you hire? All right . . . we're getting to it.

BUT FIRST . . . A "YOU BETTER LISTEN" WARNING

Below, we'll be discussing how to find and hire the right people, but before the actual hiring takes place do your *due diligence.*

I learned in the real estate investment world that a lot of things can creep up and bite you in the wallet. In that world, the number one problem is landlord-tenant issues. Horror stories abound about bad tenants.

But the blame doesn't lie with the tenant.

The blame is squarely at the feet of the landlord . . . more specifically, the landlord who did *not* do appropriate diligence. The tenant lied and you didn't check.

It's a harsh reality, gang.

People LIE!

And if people lie to become a tenant . . . they will lie to become an employee.

Potential employees will lie about everything: past work history, current work history, personal history, education history and so on. They will lie to suit their needs. It's all the rage now to put in bogus resumes to potential employers in order to get a position.

I knew a guy who bullshitted his way through his interviews to get a six figure job. His prior background? He was a *very* good used car salesman. He employed those same tactics to get his new job. It took them six months to catch on, but the point is he got hired and paid for those six months.

Don't think it can't happen to you.

How to Do Due Diligence

No matter what someone's resume says, no matter how nice they are, no matter how good looking they are . . . check them out completely.

You think I'm kidding? I'm not.

Find out:

- Do they drink?
- Take drugs?
- Have a criminal record?
- Been fired in the past?
- Been dishonorably discharged from the military?
- Are they a head case?
- Too meek, too hard?
- Are they willing to submit to drug testing?

- Can they provide proof of any stated education?

You get the point. You should identify the traits you are looking for in an ideal employee and work from there.

I suggest that you do an extensive background check for employment history and criminal background as well.

I hope that we are in agreement that it is **always** best to nip a potential problem in the bud. Do not ignore your instincts or give in to your needs. Keep your eyes open and as Ronald Regan said, "Trust, but verify."

Nuff said...back to hiring.

Who NOT to Hire

Do not hire family and or friends.

Hey, it's only my opinion. But the odds are that at some point, something will go wrong, and possibly very wrong. If you want to preserve the relationship, it is best not even to put yourself in the position.

Do you want to have to fire your brother-in-law? Your sister? Your uncle? Some relationships are worth preserving, so don't put them at risk.

Do not hire someone just because they're "looking for a job."

Too many business owners do this. They hire anyone for anything.

Can you believe it?

Instead, you need to hire the very **best** person for the job who is willing to accept what you're willing to pay them. And you might be interested to know that you may have to pay a little more to get the **best**. But it's worth it.

The people who are the **best** at something don't come cheap.

Remember, "buy cheap, buy twice," or in this case, "hire cheap, hire twice."

It's not good enough to hire someone who will just "get by" in a position you need filled. Verify that they have the necessary skills to do their job well.

Pretend you're looking for a date.

Not just any date, you're looking for **THE** date. The one who will turn heads, make your friends jealous, and your mom proud.

You want quality, and it's out there.

Forrest Gump

What are the intangibles you are looking for? Hopefully you've identified the skill set needed but this is different. What in addition to that skill set would make this a great hire.

Not good hire . . . a **great** one.

Forrest Gump is one of my favorite movies. Maybe one of yours too. If so, you will remember the scene when he told his beloved Jenny, "I'm not a smart man." Sorry Forrest, but I disagree. You **were** a smart man. A **very** smart man. Why?

BECAUSE YOU FOLLOWED INSTRUCTIONS!!!!!

Yes, Forrest followed instructions all throughout the movie and he ended out on top every time.

He . . . paid . . . attention.

That's who we want, Forrest Gump. And if you can't hire Forrest, hire someone like Forrest who can and will *follow instructions*.

This is where it all begins gang.

So let's throw out some bait.

Wherever you should choose to advertise, I would suggest that you place an ad with clear yet potentially confusing instructions.

Confusing instructions?

I know. This may sound a bit odd, but it goes to how well someone can follow instructions. Most people tend to gloss over instructions and figure that they've "got it" with a quick glance.

Unfortunately, in the business world, that "quick glance" can end up costing you a lot of money.

Here is a cool example of following or not following instructions. As a matter of fact, it was such a powerful lesson for me, I have never forgotten it.

I was in sixth grade, yes, that long ago, and we were given a pop quiz. Don't you just love those? Anyway, the quiz was twenty questions long, multiple choice, and a twenty minute time limit to complete.

When the quiz was handed out, the teacher *emphasized* that we were to read instructions before beginning.

At the top of the quiz were the words, "Read Instructions Before Beginning."

I wasn't prepared for the pop quiz.

Everyone knew they were under a time limit.

As I worked through the problems, I was surprised. It was a pretty easy quiz. For me, this was good news. I was not the sharpest tool in the shed and I needed all the good grades I could get.

I blew through that quiz, feeling pretty confident that I'd aced it. Then I got to the last question.

Huh?

It wasn't a question. It was a statement. It said, "If you have reached this final paragraph, you have failed the quiz. The instructions told you to *NOT* answer any questions."

Yikes!

A big fat "F" all because I was in a rush, and I assumed that instructions on a pop quiz could not possibly be important.

I have never forgotten that lesson.

As I said earlier, in the business world, this can be disastrous. Imagine placing a $20,000 media buy with specific instructions as to when the spot times should be only to find out the sales rep "didn't pay attention." That could blow your entire campaign. Not only do your employees need to be able to follow very specific instructions, you need to be sure that *anyone* you are dealing with can follow them.

I kind of got ahead of myself there but I wanted to be clear that when hiring someone, they need to be able to "do your bidding" so be sure to test before you buy.

Free Thinking (within reason)

So, what else are we looking for? Personally, I like free thinkers, but not too free. What I mean is that I do not want a mindless drone, of which there seems to plenty of these days. I want some-one with a little bit of creativity.

Here is an example of how this can fit with any employee.

I had an accountant for years who was just a great guy. He was very good and kept me out of trouble. Eventually however, my business had gotten so big and was bringing in so much money that he actually came to me and said that he felt it was time to step aside as things may be getting too big for him.

I appreciated his honesty and we parted on good terms.

I then went out a hired a highly referred CPA who specialized in small business owners. At our first meeting he asked for a copy of my past few years tax returns so he could review them. I wasn't quite sure why he wanted to do that but I didn't question him.

About a week later I received a call from him and he asked me if I would like him to re-do the returns. I asked why, and he informed me that my accountant did a good job . . . a good job for the IRS! He said that the returns were done in an **ultra**-conservative manner and that my previous accountant did me no favors at all by performing in that manner.

I was shocked.

My accountant, who probably thought he was looking out for me was actually hurting me by not pushing the envelope and taking advantage of things that could **legally** be taken advantage of. He was not acting in a creative manner at all. Instead of reaching out a bit and getting a little creative, he chose to stay exactly in the box they set out for him. The result was thousands of dollars on overpayment of taxes that I should not have paid.

Well, let's just say that we fixed that problem. My point is this, something even as mundane as accounting can use some creativity.

Appearances can be Deceiving

This is also one of the reasons I am not big on appearances of people I hire. Unless they are in a direct position of dealing with the public in a manner that "acceptable" appearance is necessary, I don't really care.

I don't care if you have piercings, tattoos, long hair, shaved head, etc. Obviously, hygiene is important but you get what I am saying. I am not concerned with publicly accepted "norms."

Many of the geeks and freaks out there are the most creative people and make some of the best employees.

Do not under any circumstances hire based just on appearance unless you are running a modeling agency or some other type of business that requires, "the look".

By the way, all you guys out there that hire some hot chick because . . . she's hot? I will say the odds are probably very high that will cost you in one way or another. Think with your wallet not your "you know what." Same goes for you ladies out there although you are clearly not as shallow as my male counterparts.

Communication over Looks . . . Every Time

Even though I am not concerned about their appearance, I am concerned with communication skills. I am a stickler for this in most cases. Again, depending on the need you have, this may not be that big of a deal. If your employee need is a floor sweeper, you probably will not need a thespian.

On the other hand, in many if not most cases, we will be looking for someone fairly literate. This is especially important with anyone who will be doing any type of phone work. People tend to equate IQ level with speech patterns and accents. Think about it, and be honest, if you hear a Southern accent, I'll bet you automatically deduct about thirty IQ points.

Right?

Obviously I am not saying to exclude anyone with an accent. As a matter of fact, rightly or wrongly, people are often prejudiced. If you hear an English accent on the other end of the phone, many people equate that with sophistication and class. On the other hand, if you hear an Indian accent, often our first response is anger because another American job has been outsourced.

Your phone people are generally the first point of contact, so be sure whoever is in that role is a fit. This is not hard, gang. We are looking for pleasant, well spoken, well-informed people who are **NOT** pushovers.

In many cases this person will be your gatekeeper.

Another very big plus would be sales skills.

What? You say your phone people aren't in sales?

You're wrong.

Everyone is in sales. Some not as obvious as others, but sales nonetheless.

These criteria should be followed for **ALL** your phone people or anyone dealing with the public. Think about this for a minute.

We are all in the "people" business. And in this business, you need to be able to navigate in such a manner that you end up with your desired result.

Here is an example.

One of my businesses is the real estate investment world. In dealing with rental properties one of the avenues I always took was subsidized housing or to use a more familiar term, Section 8 housing.

To learn more about my real estate investment training, visit, www.creatingwealth101.com.

When dealing in the subsidized housing world, you need to deal with caseworkers and inspectors who are government employees. They hate their jobs and they are miserable most of the time. They get landlords and tenants calling them all day long, yelling at them.

What you need to know is that *they* hold all the cards.

So, what was my approach? Simple, I killed them with kindness. I laid it on heavy. I told them how much I admired that they could do such a tough job and how pleased I was with their service. I would send thank you cards and sometimes even ordered pizzas for the office I was dealing with.

Guess what? I got whatever I wanted. Why is this important?

Well, if you call down there like many landlords and mouth off about your inspection being late or complaining about anything else in the process, they will put their foot on your neck so fast you won't know what hit you.

It won't be obvious, but it will happen.

An inspection that could take place in a few days is now delayed for a few weeks. This means **no rent** for however long this takes. Do you see where I am going with this?

This means *money out of your pocket.*

Sometimes we need to play the game, gang.

This is what I mean when talking about how your employees should be dealing with the public. We always want to make the public happy. When they are happy, they spend money.

When they are not happy, they don't.

Having employees who communicate well with the public is **not** a luxury for your business, it is a necessity. I don't care if you own a little coffee shop or run a manufacturing plant. All people want to know that they are understood and appreciated.

The communication between you and your employees, and your employees and the public needs to be at the top of the list.

So, hire right.

Measure and Manage

Isn't it funny how the things you that you hate doing the most are sometimes the most important? Yup, get over it.

Measuring what your employees do and more importantly, "managing" them is something most business owners dislike. They either avoid it or they do it half-assed.

That is a very expensive way to operate.

It doesn't matter if you feel you have made the best hire possible, you still must track what your employees are doing as well as "directing" them as you see fit. Many business owners simply hire someone, give a brief description as to what is expected, and then turn them loose. It is somewhat amusing at how stunned these employers are when said employee goes sideways on them.

So let's start with measuring.

As I stated earlier, communication is supremely important in the success of any business. In this case, I refer to the communication between you and your employees. In order to measure their performance, you must know what the end result should be and how long it will take.

Here is a set of clear instructions you could give to a secretary, customer service rep, etc.

"I want you to do ten-minute courtesy calls to these twenty clients, and supply me with a brief report. I need it to be done by noon."

That was very clear, right? Yes, it was. Clear, to the point, with specific instructions that you can manage.

How?

Simple math.

If the workday starts at 8:00 a.m. and lunch break is noon, you have four hours. I clearly instructed said employee to do **ten-minute** courtesy calls. These are not "Tell me your entire experience with us" calls, these are quick, "Hey how are you, we love you and wanted to make sure you love us," type calls.

20 clients x 10 min are 200 minutes. 200 minutes equals 3.3 hrs. Start at 8 am.

You can do the math.

Some of you may be saying feel this is a bit rough. The task may not even take ten minutes per call. At least 30% of the people you will not reach and have to leave voice mails. 20% will be quick calls no more than five minutes. The remaining may take the full ten minutes. This gives *plenty* of time to complete the assigned task.

"But Jim, you want them to give a report, too."

Yes, but I want the Cliffs Notes version, not *War and Peace*.

Here is my reasoning behind this. As I demonstrated with the basic math, this is a task that takes under four hours. However, what *many* business owners do is this:

"I need you get call these twenty clients and make sure everything is OK."

See any problem there?

I hope so.

If you didn't, let's just say things are a bit open ended. You can bet your sweet booty that many employees will make a full day out of this task if they are not given a *deadline.*

It's called *work*, for a reason. If you forgot the only reason to have employees, go back a few pages and refresh your memory. When you are paying someone, with *your* hard-earned money to perform a task in an efficient and timely manner, you are a fool if you do not enforce it.

Now, let's say they have that task completed in two hours, then what?

As I stated earlier, this is why it is so important *not* to hire non-thinking drones. This is why you need someone with some initiative.

This is also, once again, where communication comes in. A good line of communication will have this laid out before the task is begun.

"Oh great and wonderful boss, once I complete this task, what I can do is jump right on _____ (insert any project here), what do you think"?

See what I mean? Leave nothing open-ended. This sounds like a "self-starting" employee, but if you don't give specific instructions you might find yourself with an employee who spent the last seven hours just waiting for you to tell them what to do, or worse, they'll get involved in something you don't want them working on.

Listen, if you feel like tossing out your hard-earned money to a bunch of do-nothings, be my guest. I can tell you from firsthand experience that many employees spend their days, and your money, surfing the web, making personal phone calls, etc.

The day ends and not only has nothing been accomplished, the dummy business owner doesn't even **know** nothing has been accomplished. He is too busy putting out fires to even worry about it until it is too late.

ALL EMPLOYEES MUST BE GIVEN CLEAR, DETAILED, AND MEASURABLE TASKS

Your job as a business owner is to know the daily tasks you want to have accomplished, how long they should take, and the results you are looking for. If you cannot do that, you need to hire someone that can do it for you. I completely understand that most entrepreneurs and not good managers. I get it.

However, that does not excuse the need for management should your business have employees.

That, my friend, is *still* your job.

Big Brother is Watching

Another way to monitor what your employees are doing is by video surveillance and monitoring of computer systems.

WHAT??!! I can hear you now. "That's not fair. What do you mean track what they are doing? And watch them?"

Perhaps you are confused as to what type of enterprise you are running? Is it a "business" or is it a "charity"?

I am not going to waste any more time convincing you. I am just going to tell you what to do and let you decide.

Ignore me at your own risk.

Step one is to get your hands on any one of a number of services or software that will allow you to view in real time, exactly what your employee is doing at any given moment, from any location. You will also be able to view past visiting places they may have wandered onto. You can literally track, minute by minute.

Video surveillance is another tracking method that thankfully seems to be more prevalent these days.

Listen, you ARE being watched. Like it or not.

For God's sake they were able to catch the punks who did the Boston bombing within a few days just by video feeds from department stores. Forget whether you feel it is right or wrong.

It just IS!

I also strongly endorse it for watching employees.

As much as you may not want to believe it, sometimes people go bad. Workplace theft is ridiculously high in this country. If you happen to be the owner of that business, guess who pays the freight?

If you are thinking that these measures will be detrimental to your employee's attitude I beg to differ.

When are you on your best behavior?

When someone is watching.

If you have employees who really want to keep their job, and they know they are being watched and tracked, it is probably a safe bet that they will perform.

Environment and Pay

Speaking of your employees being happy or unhappy let's discuss workplace environment and pay structure.

Workplace environment. Listen, much of this is common sense. You obviously want to "within reason" do things and or provide environment and circumstances that keep employees happy.

Key phrase, "within reason."

A workplace is a workplace. I know that the current trend is to have these incredible facilities that cater to their every need, which in turn makes them a happy-happy, joy-joy employee who kicks ass and stays forever. It seems the hippie movement is still alive and well.

That looks good on paper, but I know that not to be the case.

I have two close friends who happen to work for a company that was recently voted the best work environment in the country. They beat out the legendary GOOGLE facility. I have been to this facility and I can tell you that it is truly a sight to see. I mean it is a fantasyland with everything you could imagine from movie theaters, to coffee shops to restaurants to dry cleaners and on and on. I am not easily impressed but I can say that I was blown away. I have been to many of the top luxury resorts in the world and none of them had anything on this place.

I am not going to name the company as they're a multi-billion dollar "privately" held company and I don't want to get sued for what I am about to say.

They provide an unbelievable fantasyland for employees.

But as with most fantasies, it doesn't last.

Word is that most employees last only three years. I won't get into the reasons. The point is, the "feel good" work environment is not in any way shape or form a guarantee of employee productivity.

I am not advocating Spartan work conditions, but I also do not recommend going out of your way to create a workplace that will have your employees singing *Kumbaya* every day.

The basics are the obvious. Clean and safe. I also prefer an environment that stimulates some creativity but that is your call. Also, depending on your business, you can add to "clean and safe" as you feel needed. Again however, I have seen firsthand that workplace extravagance does not equal a positive outcome. It may help, but it is certainly not the be all end all.

Proper Care and Feeding

Just a joke.

You see, I live in a zoo. Not really, but close. My daughter, Natalie, is the animal whisperer and she whispers to them to come to our house. Chickens, horses, dogs, gerbils, lizards, and spiders . . . you name it. Anyway, all animals should have proper care and feeding.

So should employees.

Feeding, they're on their own. Yes, that was a joke too.

But care . . . that is a different issue. When I say care, I am talking about their compensation. Compensation that is fair. Not too much, not too little and with the potential for "earned rewards."

Emphasis on "earned."

We live in an entitlement society and I don't see any signs of that ever changing anytime soon. This has spilled over to many segments of society, including employees.

This all began with Andrew Carnegie and his workforce at U.S. Steel.

He **WAS** the only game in town and took it to the extreme. His workers were overworked and underpaid. They believed that because he was making so much money, he should "share the wealth."

And so it began . . .

I won't bother with a history lesson about the advent of workforce unionization. You can see the results for yourself.

Refocus. You must clearly understand that employee compensation is a **business** transaction. As the owner of that business you alone will determine this:

How much money is going to GO in and STAY IN your pocket?

Your employee or future employee has everything **BUT** that, at the forefront of their mind.

They don't care about you.

Sorry to say that, but it is true.

YOU are a necessary evil for them. *YOU* are their adversary. And frankly, that is good. There needs to be a very clearly drawn line in the sand that identifies who is boss and who is not.

So the idea is to keep as much profit as we can, what we pay, and how do we do it.

I am not going to tell you what to pay, as you should base that on your industry standards. And I've already told you that I will pay *more* for the right person.

I am a highly paid consultant for good reason . . . I'm good . . . REAL good. Sure, you could find many people cheaper, but not anywhere near the value I bring. Price and value are two different things.

You can find out about my business consulting programs at **www.CreatingWealth101.com**.

This approach will be helpful in determining your pay scale. Don't give away the store, but don't miss the long-term benefit and intangibles the right person can bring to the table.

I also strongly recommend that you pay very generous, performance and results base bonuses.

Note I said "performance and results based."

Most employees at some point develop an entitlement rather than an ownership mentality, feeling that time served and company profits should correlate into more money for them, earned or not. You see this with unions and especially the teachers union.

I also recommend public recognition of a job well done. Everyone likes a good pat on the back every once in a while especially when it is in front of others. Good for the ego.

You may think that this is counter to what I said earlier about having a no nonsense work place but it isn't. To be profitable, you don't need to run a sweatshop or be a dictator.

What you do want is to run your business with a firm hand and clear guidelines.

Your employees work better when they are allowed to excel, be recognized, appreciated, and rewarded for it. You do this because they **earned** it.

The employee/owner relationship is adversarial enough without them hating your guts because you do not appreciate their **good** work. Sometimes a good pat on the back and an "atta-boy" will go a long way.

CHAPTER 4

You're Going to Get Sued

isclaimer: I am not an attorney, thank God. And I am not giving legal advice. Leave that to those less competent. I am offering my opinion based on my past experiences. You should always consult with legal counsel before entering into a legal battle. I guess.

Getting Sued

Who me?

Yes, you.

If you are in business for any length of time, the odds are very strong that you will be involved in some type of litigation.

It may come from a disgruntled employee, a vendor, a customer, a partner, the government, or any one of hundreds of places.

Remember, the question is not *if*, it is **when**.

I've become very disenchanted with the world we live in when it comes to this matter. There seems to zero personal responsibility being accepted and everyone wants a free ride with you as the one who is going to pay for it.

I don't like it, but this is real and needs to be dealt with.

Not only is this issue very real, it is **very** scary. You could have the unlimited powers of the government breathing down your neck due to an anonymous tip from a competitor, disgruntled employee, or whomever.

The very scary part is that **truth** has very little to do with these types of investigations. I'll get to that in a bit.

I will begin this section with apologies to my personal friend and attorney as well as a few other attorneys I am friendly with. They are, for the most part, the exceptions to what has become a very dirty business.

And that's putting it mildly.

There is very good reason people have been complaining about lawyers for hundreds of years.

Don't believe me?

Check out a couple of quotations about lawyers and see if you don't agree with me now.

~

The first thing we do – Let's kill all the lawyers.

- King Henry VI, Act IV, Scene II, William Shakespeare

~

I don't think you can make a lawyer honest by an act of legislature.

You've got to work on his conscience,

and his lack of conscience is what makes him a lawyer.

~Will Rogers

~

See what I mean?

You will not find this to be unusual. Most entrepreneurs have a very, very strong dislike for lawyers. You'll get no argument from me on that. But sometimes they are a necessary evil.

I will give you some tips on how to avoid lawsuits and attorneys. Sometimes there is just no choice but to have one in your corner.

No Replacement for YOUR Business Education

Before I get to that, I want to make it very clear how very important it is for you to educate yourself on any and all business subjects. Personal as well, but for the purpose of this section, business.

You must have a well-rounded education of what you can or cannot do in certain circumstances. It is very dangerous and very expensive to just blindly trust an attorney. I'm not saying it cannot work out for you, I am saying it is a crapshoot with the odds stacked against you.

Here is what I mean.

Years ago, in my real estate investment training business, my partner and I had a number of employees who provided various services to our clients. Well, as is almost always the case, one of these people decided that he was smarter than the rest of us and figured that he could steal our real estate training protocol and marketing strategies, and go into competition.

That is what he did.

Behind our backs.

We didn't even realize what happened until we heard radio ads that sounded like ours.

We immediately went on the attack and went for a consultation with a very well-known business attorney in Pittsburgh.

Heads up!
What I am going to share with you in the following pages were things I did not know at the time.
You will get the benefit of my pain.

Anyway, we sat with this attorney.

ALL DAY.

He quizzed us on every aspect of our business, including how much we made as far as income. Can you guess why he wanted to know how much we made? In case you can't, it was so he knew how much he could soak us for.

By day's end, we had made no progress and received a $2,400.00 bill to boot.

For *one day*!

He convinced us that it would be in our best interest and in the best interest of our business to hire him as this would require "lots of research." This struck me as odd as I was sure this was not a unique circumstance to businesses.

But, given our ignorance, we hired him.

A few later weeks later, I was telling this story to one of my business associates who had a similar issue in his business. He informed me that he was quite sure that there was nothing we could do to stop our new competitor as we did not have, nor did we create, anything unique.

We did not "invent" real estate investing per se, so we could not claim it as our own.

By this time, we are into this "reputable, skilled" attorney for an additional $5,000.

At our next meeting, I relayed to this attorney what my friend had told me. My jaw dropped when he answered that my friend was correct. We did not invent the real estate investment business so therefore we could not claim it as solely ours.

He KNEW!

At our very first meeting he knew that there was nothing we could do yet he continued to play the game and bill us.

Almost $8,000 later we know we had been worked.

Here's the sick part.

That is what they do.

To him, he did nothing wrong. His defense to us was that he was going to see what he could do to stop our competitor, even though he **knew** he could not.

Always be aware of the animal you are dealing with. If I had had some knowledge on the subject, I could have asked better questions. But I didn't and neither did my partner.

We blindly trusted and got beat.

I would advise you that before you contract any attorney for any issue, you try to bring yourself up to speed on the subject so you can ask the right questions before it's too late. With the Internet today, you have access to the answers to almost any question you can think of. Use it.

How to Avoid Getting Sued

How do you avoid and or settle a potential suit? There are two sides to this fence that we need to examine. Are you being attacked or are you the one doing the attacking?

Let's start with you being on the attack.

Let me be clear that if at all possible, *always* avoid a fight. It's cheaper in the long run. However, if you are forced to fight, I recommend you fight and fight hard! I mean **really** hard, to the point that your opponent thinks you are a raving lunatic.

Always remember the name of the game you are in, and in this game, it is to **win**. Period! Forget about being nice, hurting feelings and so forth. You do what you need to do to win, and get out as cheaply as possible. This is easier said than done, which is why you need to know how to run the game.

OK. So you are on the attack.

This could come from someone or something attempting to hurt you or your business. This can range from extortion of an ex-employee, theft of intellectual property, copyright infringement etc.

Here are the steps to stop this in its tracks:

- Once the party in question has been identified, along with their violation, you need to send them a strongly worded letter and copy your attorney on this letter. At this juncture, we are trying to get out of the situation without hiring an attorney. This letter needs to be very strongly worded informing them that you are aware of what they have done or are in the process of doing.
- You then *clearly* instruct them to cease and desist in said activity.
- Then, you outline what you are prepared to do to them should they choose to ignore your demand.
- You also want to put a deadline for their compliance.
- Have the letter delivered certified so they need to sign it.

My reason for this strategy is the knowledge of human nature.

Most people don't have the guts for all-out war. Not someone who is trying to rip you off or extort you. I think you will find this to be very effective on many occasions.

If someone thinks you are willing to go to any lengths to stop them *and* damage them, they will more than likely stop.

Especially if they are a bad guy.

Time to Bring in the Attorneys

Should this tactic not be effective, you will need to bring in the attorneys.

Pay attention here!

YOU need to be actively involved in whatever suit you are in, and **YOU** need to be able to dictate to your attorney what you think should be done.

Many people are uncomfortable with this. They have the notion that they are inferior to their attorney. As a non-attorney, they feel they are not qualified to question their attorney or make suggestions to them as to what course of action they want to take.

Guess what will happen. If you engage an attorney, but do **not** participate, plan on spending a hell of a lot of money. Please, take my advice on this one.

If you are at the point where an attorney is needed, be sure you have the right guy on your team. I have seen $200.00/hour attorneys who could wipe the floor with $800.00/hour guys and I have seen both $200.00/hour and $800.00/hour guys not worth a plugged nickel.

You need to interview your potential partner, I mean attorney, in this case.

If you already have an attorney, make sure he is the right kind of attorney for your case. A real estate attorney will do you little good in a criminal case.

If you do not have an attorney, or have the wrong kind of attorney, the best way to find one is recommendations from friends or business associates.

Be wary of hiring an attorney simply because of their marketing powers.

Interview at least three of your referrals.

Don't be surprised if you're charged for the consultation. I have no problem with that. Just be sure to get the fee being charged up front so you are not surprised.

Now it is your turn to grill them. Do **not** be intimidated. Treat this as if you are interviewing a potential employee for an important position, which is exactly what it is. You're bringing someone onto your business team.

You need to lead the conversation.

I have seen attorneys who charge by the hour for consultations that drag out the process with moronic questions just to keep the meter running. You take the lead.

Here are some questions you should ask:

- What do you charge, and what are your billing procedures? Are you going to charge me every time I speak to you even for five minutes? (I have seen some crazy bills...down to the minute. I believe they call that gouging.)
- How long have you been practicing?
- What is your expertise?
- What do you feel are your strengths and weaknesses?
- How aggressive are you?
- How successful have you been in previous cases? (We are looking for outcomes here.)

- Have you had *similar* cases to mine and what was the outcome and timeline?
- What is the biggest case you ever had and outcome?
- Have you ever been disciplined by the Bar Association?
- Have you ever been sued?
- Have you ever fired clients, is so why?
- Have clients ever fired you, is so why?
- Can you provide references of clients with similar cases?
- How attentive will you be to my case and how accessible will you be to me?
- Are you willing to use any *legal* means necessary even though it may seem out of the norm or a bit extreme? (I will explain this question shortly.)
- What do you estimate as far as a timeline and billing amount to get this case resolved? (This can be hard for them to answer due to variables and due to them not wanting to commit to a fee. Ask anyway.)

These questions, should give you a pretty good idea if you have the right guy or girl for your team.

I have a tip for you – do not underestimate female attorneys. I have seen some killers that I would have loved to have on my team.

Now that we have the right people on the right bus, it's time to go to work.

We are still talking about *YOU* being on the attack right now.

"Any Legal Means Necessary"

The reason for the question about "using any legal means necessary" is this. The first thing we are going to want our attorney to do is file what is known as a Discovery Motion.

Always keep at the forefront what the objective is, and the objective is to *WIN* and *WIN FAST*.

A Discovery Motion is something many attorneys may be unwilling to do at first.

It's a big bomb to drop.

However, if the case has the possibility of you recovering monetary damages, you are permitted to have this motion filed.

We are going to tear into the life of our opponent. They will be hit with mounds of questions that will dig into their personal and business life. It's not pretty.

People don't like having their personal business aired in public. Their unknowing spouses like it even less. On more than one occasion I have had the sheriff serve opponents at their home or place of employment. There is nothing worse than seeing a police car pulling up to your front door.

When you adopt this strategy, you could put an immediate end to the case.

It is amazing how quickly you get someone's attention and how quickly he or she changes attitude once this bomb is dropped.

Our goal is to end it quickly and inexpensively and this will more than likely do the trick. If it does not, you need to aggressively continue in order to get your desired result.

I think that you will find however that just threatening, and threatening in a *BIG* way will often be enough to end a fight before it really begins.

Under Attack – You're Getting Sued

Now let's look at things from the perspective of you being attacked or sued.

Yes, it will happen and you will probably be shocked. Get over it. It's the cost of doing business. When this happens, the first thing you need to determine is *WHY*. Why is someone or some entity coming after you?

For instance, if you are in some type of personal service business that offers refunds and for some reason you refuse to issue such refund, don't be surprised if you get sued.

Here is my advice for you on that issue:

NEVER, EVER, EVER, refuse to issue a refund, even if you are in the right.

This is a tough pill to swallow but in the end it will be cheaper. I have seen iron-clad contracts in favor of a service provider be ignored in a court of law. Never ever assume you have a contract that protects you from lawsuits.

If you can settle, do it and do it fast.

The other important aspect to consider is that as much as you may not want to admit it, *YOU* may be in the wrong. You also open yourself up to a public trashing on the Internet and that can cost you big time in the form of lost future business. I see many business owners crossing into this danger zone of not issuing re-funds even if they are in the wrong. Don't go down that road.

So you have been attacked and it is not a refund issue, but something that is completely out of the blue. It is also very likely that you are the real victim. What do you do? Personally, I follow the same strategy. You go on the attack. There is an old saying, "The best defense, is a strong offense."

I have found this to be true.

I will restate what I said earlier that most people do not have the guts for a knock-down drag-out fight, especially if they know they are not in the right. Go on the offense and hit them hard. I have used this with great success many times in the past, often without the assistance of an attorney.

Don't be a victim.

If you truly did something wrong, do whatever you need to correct it and move on as quickly and inexpensively as possible. If it is you being attacked, stand and fight and fight hard. We are talking about your livelihood here. Most of the general public, including business owners, would never adopt these types of tac-tics as it is generally considered out of the "norm."

Nonsense! I think that is a big mistake.

Bottom line: Use whatever you need to win.

One-Legged Man in an Ass-Kicking Contest

I wanted to start this very important section with a bit of levity because what follows may be one of the most frightening things you will ever encounter. It is not fun, or funny. It is deadly serious.

READ this part very carefully.

On any given day, the average business owner knowingly or unknowingly violates any number of government laws and or regulations. Many of these may go unnoticed. However, they do not "have" to be noticed.

As each day goes by, more and more entrepreneurs and business owners are being investigated and harassed by the government. This can be anything from regulatory commissions, State Attorney Generals, the IRS and, worst of all, the FBI.

It is imperative that you understand the power they hold over you and your business.

It is virtually unlimited and fairness is not in the equation.

The truth also takes a back seat. Do not make the fatal mistake of thinking that this cannot happen to you. I don't care how nice a person you are, how much you do for your community, what a good business owner you are. None of that matters. All that matters is that you are in their sights and you better strap in.

How do you end up in their sights?

Lots of ways.

Consumer complaints, competitors making anonymous tips to the IRS, bouncing a check, exclusions on your tax returns, and on and on and on . . .

If and when, you find yourself in their sights, it is time to follow a different strategy. I know I spoke earlier about fighting to win but this is not a battle that you will win. It's not fair, I know, but it is what it is.

You. Will. Not. Win.

You're not going to win, unless of course your ideal of winning is spending thousands of dollars in attorney's fees. If you are innocent, don't just roll over, but be warned, that you will not get off scott free. Remember, they have the bigger stick so the idea is to get out with the "least" amount of damage possible. As a side note, and I will reiterate this soon, *NEVER, EVER*, be sweet talked or coerced into meeting with any law enforcement agency without an attorney. *NEVER!* Even if you feel you have done nothing wrong and even if they tell you it's just for a little "chat". Don't do it.

When someone contacts you such as the IRS, Attorney General or FBI, you need to be very careful in how you make your first move. Especially if this is of the criminal ilk.

The strategy is to be polite, courteous, and non-confrontational. *DO NOT*, however, talk to them *WITHOUT* an attorney . . . and a *GOOD* one.

Remember, fairness has nothing to do with issues such as this and you could be completely innocent, but it doesn't matter.

When you are searching and interviewing attorneys for your business, I also recommend that you get referrals for *VERY* good criminal attorneys just to have their name ready and available.

Did it scare you that I said "criminal"? It should.

As I said, there are many seemingly innocent errors that can launch a criminal investigation. Most people think of criminal as the bad guy with the gun. Not the case. There are thousands of "crimes" included in Federal statutes and they are very broad.

Remember your idea of a crime and what the Federal Government thinks is a crime are two different things.

When these investigations begin, all fairness is out the window. You need to know that you are in for a tough battle. You do have rights, which are basically the Fifth and Sixth Amendment.

Meaning you *have* the right to an attorney and the **right** to remain silent.

During the course of any investigation there will be things that may happen that will rattle you to the core. This is why you must have the very best attorney that you can afford on your team.

You need someone who **KNOWS** what can and cannot be done *to* you and *by* you.

I say this because there **WILL** be things happen that strain the limits of common sense and decency; especially if you are a good, law abiding citizen who in your mind has done nothing wrong. And maybe you haven't, but you may be treated as if you have.

I'm not going to sugar coat this.

Your business, personal life, and reputation can all be destroyed.

It has happened to bigger people than you.

I am going to leave it with this bit of advice. You need to run your business with the utmost integrity.

You need to keep **EXTREMELY** accurate records of everything you do. You need to surround yourself with experts in your business: the right attorney, CPA, etc.

Should you find yourself under investigation, you must be completely honest and not try and hide or obstruct any investigation, and you must follow your Attorneys council. You need to stay focused on getting the best possible outcome you can get.

As I said, this will not be fun.

But, you will get through it.

You may be a bit bloodied, but a true entrepreneur will get through it. If you have done nothing wrong and are being unjustly accused, stand tall, keep moving forward with the knowledge that this too shall pass and you can pick up the pieces and move on.

If on the other hand you have committed wrongdoing or even worse, intentional wrong doing, well then, there is not much I can say other than you get what you deserve. If you're one of the bad guys, you will get caught, with prison being a not too uncommon outcome for the perpetrator.

In business as well as life it's not always pretty and it's not always fair.

Deal with it.

Run your business with the utmost integrity. If and when the storm comes, deal with it and move on.

That's what entrepreneurs do.

Some Questions for Your Criminal Lawyer

Many of the questions you had for your business lawyer will apply but there a few additional questions you need to ask:

1. Have they ever been part of a Federal Investigation?
2. What type and what was the outcome?

3. How much experience do they have with these types of cases?

4. How many or these cases were white-collar crime and how many were criminal?

5. Can they give you a good idea of how the case/investigation is going to unfold?

6. Can I continue to operate my business and how do I protect any further damage to my business and reputation during the investigation?

7. What is your experience with plea-bargaining in cases like this? What were the outcomes?

8. What is the worst-case scenario I could be looking at?

That last question is one that many people really don't want to know the answer to but in my opinion, it is better to know the worst thing that can happen rather than sitting and worrying yourself sick day and night over what may or may not happen.

HOT TIP

If at all possible, seek out council that has been previously part of a Federal organization. Many former attorneys of these agencies move on to private practice and know the ins and outs of what can and cannot happen. I liken this to having an accountant who formerly worked for the IRS as an auditor

Get the best people for your team. It may be more expensive, but more than worth it in the long run.

CHAPTER 5

Partnerships

Partnership is the worst ship to sail.

~My Father-In-Law

Aye matey, and so it is.

What is the phrase the kids use today? OMG!

Yeah, OMG. I could write some scary stuff in this chapter, but I'll try and keep it tame in an effort for all you out there with a partner from taking a bridge.

It's a funny thing how everyone seems to feel that they need partners when going into business for themselves. I guess it's a security issue; meaning an internal security.

That is not a knock on anyone as I was dumb enough to do it not once, but twice!

I will put this as simply as I can:

DONT DO IT!!!

Seriously, don't do it. My big mistake in the failed partnerships I had is the same mistake that many entrepreneurs make. We tend to look at people and situations not as they truly are, but as we would like them to be.

In my case, I had always been a very trusting person. Take note of my use of the past tense "had."

In the past, I liked to believe what people told me. I liked to believe they would do nothing to harm me. And I liked to believe that they were as competent as they told me they were. All of the above and much more, came back to bite me on my two failed attempts.

I say "bite", but *eviscerate* may be more accurate.

I am not going to get into the gory details but I will tell you that it cost me hundreds of thousands of dollars as well as very close relationships because of these partnerships.

The truth about partnerships is that they rarely succeed, and I mean rarely.

I know, I know, YOU are one of those rarities.

(I hope you are, but I highly doubt it.)

With this in mind, if you are not already in a partnership, it is best to plan for the breakup before it happens. I will discuss later what to do if you are already in the trap . . . I mean, partnership.

The Rules

Whenever we begin a new business venture, it's kind of like that new girlfriend or boyfriend. Everything is great and everything is going to stay great.

Right?

That is how we naturally tend to look at things; especially entrepreneurs who are naturally **over**-optimistic. And we hope that turns out to be the case.

But, in business as is in life, sometimes things go sideways.

What that means is *you know what* hits the fan. That is what you need to be ready for. Can you picture in your mind what's happening?

Yeah.

It's messy and all over everyone. Where do you think that phrase came from? So we start with **clear** expectations and rules that will be spelled out in what is known as an Operating Agreement.

If there were a Ten Commandments of business, and I am sure that somewhere there probably is, one of the ten would have to be.

THOU SHALL NOT EVER, EVER, ENGAGE IN ANY TYPE OF PARTNERSHIP WITHOUT AN OPERATING AGREEMENT

The results of ignoring this commandment can and most likely will be ugly.

Trust me, I know.

An Operating Agreement basically contains the rules of the company. It spells out who is responsible for what, who gets what and what happens when we fall out of love and or someone screws up real bad and we want to dissolve the company and/or partnership.

You already know that I don't like using attorneys. But, as much as I hate using them, I recommend that for this, you use one.

You and your partner can sit down in advance and lay out some ground rules and have your attorney can help with the rest. On a side note, always do as much work as possible yourself instead of letting an attorney start from scratch.

I am warning you.

Begging you.

Threatening you

DO NOT go into any business partnership without this agreement. When the time comes that it is clear things are not working and you need to get out.

You need to get out . . . and fast.

Be sure that you have any dissolution clause be made **VERY** clear, as this will help buffer the animosity and negativity that will occur. Get out as professionally and cleanly as possible.

Don't get into a battle.

When it's over: IT IS OVER!

Do whatever you have to do to get out in one piece. Are you wondering why I started with the end? Don't worry, you can thank me later.

Things to Consider

Now that I have probably convinced you that your partnership is going to end in disaster, let's talk about how to prevent that from happening. As I said, the Operating Agreement defines the rules of the company.

We talked about getting out. Let's talk about getting in.

Here are a few things to consider before you finalize your partnership with anyone:

1. Who owns what? If you are smart, you will fight and fight very hard for majority ownership of your new company. This also applies in any type of joint venture or merger. You should always want to maintain the upper hand in the ownership department. I would start at demanding 75% ownership. Yes, demand it. Scream for it. Fight for it. It *IS* that important. Never, and I mean *never*, do the standard 50/50. Take 51% if you have to, but never below that.

2. What are they, the potential partners, bringing to the table? Money, talent, connections? Far too many people go into business with friends, family members, and/or acquaintances without taking a hard look at what they have that is going to put more money in your pocket. If you were going to start a new NFL team, would you go out and grab the first bunch of guys who said they wanted to play or, would you go out and scout some already proven players and pick from the best? Right? So why be any different with your biz? By the way, in a partnership, making money comes first so I would advise that any relationship you wish to keep intact does not become part of your biz. Money's one thing, friends and family are another.

3. Are the skill and or talents they bring different from yours? This is very important. You do not need a clone of yourself; you need someone who complements what you have or brings something you do not have.

4. Can they take the heat? The reality of business is that it is tough. No way around it. So can this person or persons take it when this occurs? How will they react? Do they have any past history that you can give you a look into how they may perform under fire, i.e. "stress"? You may have heard the phrase that had its origins in military circles, "I wouldn't want to be caught in a foxhole with you." This means, in the heat of the battle, back against the wall, would you want that person in your foxhole? Could you trust them to fight and have your back?

5. How "IN" are they? Dedication is always bandied about when talking about success. It is however, very true. In this ultra-competitive world, you better damn well be **VERY** dedicated and laser focused.

Early on I had a partner who brought a lot to the table He was also a lifelong friend. He was a moneymaker, aggressive, and smart. He also had a passion to become a pilot. Eventually, that passion won out and forced us to remove him from the company resulting in lawsuits and lost friendships. There is no halfway in.

The Big Five

So, you have your five things to consider before a partnership, now, here are the five items that MUST be included in your operating agreement.

1. Salaries / Distributions. This is just what you think it is. How much are we getting paid, when, and how is it being done.

2. Buy in. Otherwise known as CAPITAL CONTRIBUTION. Hey, you've got to pay to play baby. No free rides. Each member must make a Capital Contribution to get into the company.

3. Decision making. This is a biggie. Obviously, many decisions will be made on a daily basis and most people always think that their answer is the best. You need to have this in writing. Who is calling the shots? If decisions are being made by committee, which I hate, what is the process?

4. Death or disability of a partner. In the event one or more of the partners bite the dust, you need to have a plan in place to be able to keep moving forward should you choose to do so.

5. Dissolution. This is the end game and it must be planned before played.

Ready for a Shootout?

In the event that you choose not to listen to me and decide to do a 50/50, *AT LEAST* be smart enough to include the following in your operating agreement.

Believe me when I tell you that when you need to get out or rid of someone, it needs to happen and happen fast. So what we are going to do is include an exit strategy known as a Mexican Shootout. Sounds cool doesn't it?

Here is how it works:

- When things go sideways, or you fall out of love with each other, or you realize your partner is a lazy cash-sucking slob and you both want to get as far away from each other as possible, this baby will kick in.

- Each partner will write a figure on a piece of paper, (privately) and place it in a sealed envelope. *This figure is what you would be willing to pay for the ENTIRE Company*, and you or they must have access to the amount you have chosen as your figure.

- The envelopes are brought to a neutral attorney where they will be opened.

- Whoever has bid the highest amount is now the owner of the Company, and must pay the loser for their shares based on figure indicated in the losers sealed bid.

You need to be very careful and closely consider your figure before you put it on paper. This clause is not for the squeamish but it does bring things to a very quick and final end. On the flip side, you may end up with something you don't want.

So let's say you choose this route and the "winner" does not have the buyout funds. It would be a good idea to set a timeline in your agreement for how long of a grace period will be given. If the "winner" is still not able to come up with the cash in the allotted timeline, the other partner will have the option to buy at his offered amount.

Just as is the case with a real shootout, the end is quick. However, the partner without access to funding resources could be at a disadvantage.

Mediation

Here is another potential solution to resolving your partnership conflict, although I personally find it to only be effective if the people involved are *truly* interested in resolving things.

Basically, you and the partner(s) will sit with a neutral party, which is usually an attorney, and the attorney will hear both sides of the argument and attempt to mediate. I have been involved in this type of situation twice with the results being 50/50.

Worst Case Scenario

I am well aware that many things in life are far worse than a bad business deal, but being in a partnership, with no agreement, and needing to get out or get rid of someone, ranks pretty high up there. The financial and mental toll it can and will take is pretty big.

So what can you do if you are in the situation with a partner and no agreement? This is a tough one simply because there are no painless answers.

Here are a few options:

1. If you **really** want to keep the business going but **really** need to get rid of your partner(s), you can offer to buy them out. Not pretty as they will probably want far more than you can or are willing to pay.

2. Or, they can buy you out. Again, not painless as it will force you to start over and perhaps lose hard earned reputation and/or customers.

3. You can stick it out, swallow your pride, and try and keep it together. I don't really recommend this method. When you know you have cancer, you need to cut it out.

4. You can file a lawsuit. I have done this, again I don't recommend it. I am not saying you can't or won't win. What I am saying is that the real winner will be the attorneys. Most people vastly underestimate the time and money involved in a lawsuit. You will pay a high price with both.

5. You can just walk. Just say forget it, it's not worth my time, health, sanity, etc. Leave. Go. Split. Skedaddle. . . GTFO . . . however you want to put it, just get out. In many, many cases, this is the best way to go. Money is very replaceable while time and your sanity is not.

Your Best Solution

As NIKE says, "Just do it."

Jimmy says, "Just DON'T do it."

In today's day and age there is really no reason for you to need a partner. You can have advisors or key people, but partners?

No. No need for partners.

Whether you know it or not, everything you need to run a successful business is already at your fingertips. You can outsource just about everything you need and have employees, if necessary, for the rest.

Of all of the most successful people I know, not one of them have a partner. I learned my lesson the hard way, but I learned. Hopefully you won't have to learn the hard way.

I just told you what to do.

The question is . . .

Will you listen to me?

CHAPTER 6

Time, Time, Tickin', Tickin' Away

Aah yes . . .

Time Management.

Actually, it should be called Time **MIS**-management.

Time doesn't need to be managed.

You do.

So, where to begin? I know. How about a simple quiz? Are you ready? This question is worth 100 points . . .

How many hours are in a day?

"Well duh, Jim. Obviously 24."

Hmmm, OK, very good.

So it seems that the problem here is not that you do not know how many hours you have available in a day. The problem is that you have no idea what to do with them, right?

Oh, I know you *think* you know what to do, but you probably don't. And if by some chance you do, why are you not doing it?

Here's why.

You're surfing the web, talking to friends, thinking about yesterday, thinking about tomorrow, answering your phone, texting, listening to the radio, watching TV, driving around, picking your nose, kicking a can down the street . . . blah, blah, blah.

Yes, I am going to be a bit more harsh in this chapter. I can't stand to hear someone say they have "no time" or, "There just aren't enough hours in a day," or, "I just don't know where all the time goes."

As Frank Sinatra used to say, "Don't make me slug you, punk."

We **ALL** have the same amount of time.

24 hours a day.

That's it.

You know that, you passed your quiz. But that's not the issue. The issue is how you **spend** your time, so let me try and walk you through this process of "time management."

We have all heard the expression, "Time is Money," right? Well, it is. So your first step is to determine, how much you are worth.

I mean really, what **IS** your time worth?

Eight dollars an hour?

Twenty dollars an hour?

One hundred dollars an hour?

One thousand dollars an hour?

I can't tell you what **your** hourly rate should be but I can tell you that any of the above mentioned, time-wasting activities will probably not put you very high on any pay scale.

Actually, for business purposes, **any** activity that is not directly leading you in some manner to profit is completely worthless.

And when you honestly think about how much of your time you really spend on these worthless activities, I would hope it would hurt just a bit.

If you want to be in the $1,000.00 an hour range, you need to be doing activities that make you worthy of that type of dough. Rest assured that anyone making high six or seven figures is *NOT* spending their days on time/money sucking activities.

"But Jim, it's so hard. You kind of just get sucked into it."

Yeah, I know.

You want to find out what burned down, who died, and what Kim Kardashian did last night.

Hey, if that's your thing, have at it. Just don't expect the big dollar signs to come your way.

(Speaking of Kim Kardashian, say what you want about her, but you better believe that she spends every waking moment figuring out how to make more cash. She is not spending her days surfing the web wasting time. She is working very hard to get all the cash she can from the legion of drones following her every move. If you want something valuable from watching her, watch how she markets herself.)

So the trick here is not to get sucked into the time vacuum in the first place. And here is how we do it.

The late, great Jim Rohn had a *very* powerful quote regarding time management. He said, "Don't start your day before you finish it."

Did you get that? Think about it now . . .

What he is saying is don't start your day until you pre-plan what the day is going to look like. You need to do this the night or day or week before and *not* when you wake up on said day.

So whatever method of activity tracking you prefer or use, whether it be a Day-Timer, computer, whatever, you must plan your days and weeks in advance. Doing this allows you to know exactly what you should be doing and when. If followed correctly, meaning in a disciplined manner, it will also help prevent any of the so-called interruptions that leave you saying, "There aren't enough hours in the day."

What I do is prioritize things in order of importance. No rocket science there. Lots of gurus have bandied this about. What you need to do is the same. What are the *most* important items that need to be accomplished that day? Please be clear on the word *most* important.

Tip: Add Deadlines!

Surfing the web to check the latest dirt is not going to generate profit for you. But, how about upon awakening, spending thirty minutes reading a book on sales, marketing, or better yet, *this* book?

I've talked to tons of people who wonder how some people get so much done while others get nothing done.

Again, not rocket science.

They are the masters of their time.

It seems like such a simple idea, doesn't it, planning your day in advance. Prioritizing activities in order of importance, putting deadlines on tasks, etc.

Sounds good.

Sounds easy too, but as Mike Tyson once said, "Everybody has plan until they get punched in the face." Well said, Champ.

If that is the case, and it is, what is "punching us in the face" and how do we stop it?

Let's evaluate my top eight reasons people are **not** the masters of their time:

Reason #1. The Phone/Cellphone

I swear I remember a time when there was no such thing as a cell phone, and I'm pretty sure I made money back then.

Now?

Good God, forget your phone and the world ends. You are, after all, a very important person and you must be able to be reached at all times. Aah no. You're not **that** important. At least not so important that you need to be accessible every second of the day.

The scary thing about the phone is that it has brainwashed us into thinking everything that is happening is urgent in nature and we must be readily available. When was the last time you tried to go twenty-four hours without touching your phone for anything other than **scheduled** calls? How often during the day do you find yourself in the middle of an activity and you stop because your phone rings?

Even worse, how often are you meeting with someone and **their** phone rings and they stop to answer? Here is a tip for you and perhaps a warning. I will not conduct business with someone who does that. If we have a meeting set, and my time is very expensive and very scarce and someone stops to pick up a phone?

We are done.

Why?

Because just like someone being consistently late, that is a sign that they do not respect your time.

Hey, if you don't respect my time . . . bye-bye.

As I alluded to, the only phone calls you should be taking, if you are interested in maximum productivity, are "scheduled" calls.

If you have a secretary and or receptionist, that is a good start. Not only can they make sure that calls are scheduled, but they can be the all-important *gatekeeper* who shields you from unwanted and unneeded interruptions.

Your *gatekeeper* can be given a list of calls that will be accepted should they come in. Remember, you're not **that** important, so be careful not to decide to take every call.

PRIORITIZE to MONOTIZE!

Believe it or not, I just thought of that phrase.

Not bad, and also very true.

All other calls coming in **not** on the *hot* list can be dismissed, redirected, or scheduled for the future.

All this stuff is easy if you would just implement it.

Unless you are in phone sales, I see no reason for anyone to be held hostage by the phone, whether willingly or unwillingly.

Here is a valuable tip for you.

The reason most people are addicted to the phone is they feel they will "miss" something or "lose" a deal or business.

The reality is this. Your clients and the public can easily be conditioned to follow the rules that **you** set forth. Believe it or not, you can actually tell people when you accept calls and when you will return calls. You can also tell them what "type" of calls will or will not be accepted. You can also tell them that you **never** accept incoming calls unless pre-scheduled.

Guess what?

For the most part, they will listen.

Stop worrying about missing something or upsetting someone. Train people to adapt to the way you want to do business. It really is that simple.

Reason #2: The Internet

Wow, that thing is a mousetrap if there ever was one. Crack cocaine has got nothing on the internet.

Frankly, I am still in a bit of turmoil over the internet.

On one hand, it is an awesome source of instant information. When you think about the time that can be saved and the resources you have at your disposal it is pretty impressive.

Now on the **other** hand, it can be and frequently is the biggest time suck ever created. I don't know the exact stats, but I know that a frighteningly large amount of time is spent by average workers spend surfing the web, **on their boss's dime!**

To me, that is no different than theft.

And if you're the boss and you are spending your time on the web, you're stealing from yourself.

I am of the opinion that there is a mass brainwashing of the population taking place.

I am not alone in this opinion.

This brainwashing, being conducted by government, media, and the web, more specifically Google, is designed to drive your thoughts and action to the avenues of their bidding.

From a cultural standpoint, I find it to be horrifying.

From a business standpoint, I find it to be potentially fatal.

Google's slogan of "Don't do evil" is way beyond laughable. They are one of the dirtiest, sneakiest players in the game and they want *your* money. They know that when they get your attention, they can get your money.

Every minute you spend online that doesn't directly correspond with your business is money out of your pocket. If you gave an honest assessment of how much time you waste each day online and on the phone, I think you might be stunned.

I hope so at least.

If you are in an online business, which many people are, go ahead have at it.

If you are not, you need to keep yourself in check.

I promise you, if something *big* happens, you will find out.

You don't need to have your face buried online all day.

Reason #3: Unscheduled Interruptions

The term is *Time Vampires.*

I'm sure you've heard that before but if not, I am sure you get it. This is more frequent within an office setting, especially if you are the boss.

Everyone wants you for five minutes, "Really, Boss, just five minutes." The problem is everyone's five minutes add up fast. I'm amused by the "open door policy" being implemented by so many organizations.

Open doors mean open season in my book.

Open season on *your* time.

I strongly recommend that you have a very clear policy with your employees regarding their access to you and your time. This is easier with smaller companies but also easily accomplished with larger companies as well.

I am a big fan of the "closed door" policy.

When your door is closed, you can focus on what is really important, which is marketing your business. And this is where the majority of your time *should* be spent.

If, however, you are of the "open door" philosophy at least control the situation. If you are going to allow someone to walk into your office, unscheduled, asking for "just five minutes," here is what I suggest.

First, ask the level of importance of the issue. Let them know that your day is packed and you can only deal with issues that are a 9 or 10 on a scale of 1 to 10. Ask them directly, "Is this a 9 or 10?"

Put it back on them.

Make them think twice before taking your time. Any issues that are not on that level can be put off until later.

Next, ask if this issue can be dealt with by anyone other than you.

If there *is* only you, be sure the issue is a 9 or 10. I also want them to bring not only the issue, but a potential solution. You want your employees to be able to think for themselves and not have to bug you with things they should be able to handle on their own. You need them to understand that they have permission to deal with certain issues.

So, don't bring a problem without a solution.

Lastly, if they "must" have five minutes, then they have *just* five minutes. That's it, five minutes.

People use five minutes as more of an expression than an actual timeline. Unless otherwise directed, five minutes is rarely five minutes. So if someone needs the five minutes, we set the clock. "This sounds so mean, Jim." No, it sounds smart.

Get to the crux of the issue, without any filler, and move on. It is as simple as that.

This also applies to your employees. "Water cooler" talk should be renamed, "Bleed my bank account talk." When employees are "shooting the breeze" they are not doing what they are being paid to do. (Please refer back to the employee chapter and re-read the Measure and Manage part.)

Any managers, middle managers, administrative assistants or anyone in a position where people will want to talk with them, need to implement the above strategy. I am not discounting any issues that are below a 9 or 10, I am just saying that those can be delegated or pushed back. Many times those issues are, and should be, dealt with by the managers or middle managers.

Reason #4: Meetings

There is a reason for the phrase, "Death by Meeting."

This is very similar to Reason #3 above and the solution is very similar too. I hate meetings and I make it very clear to anyone who wants a meeting with me that I hate meetings.

I also make it clear that there will be a very clear agenda and timeline and neither of these will be altered.

I understand that there is certainly a time and place for meetings. I understand the importance of meetings. I also clearly understand the misuse of meetings.

Our society has become so dependent on hand-holding that you need to have a meeting about going to the bathroom.

So, if and when you are going to have a meeting, here are the guidelines:

- Set a clear start and finish time and do not waver from it.

- Make sure everyone involved is aware of this.

- Next be sure to have clear agenda that you are ready to tackle immediately upon the start of the meeting.

- Keep a clock in a prominent place and make sure everyone is well aware of the time remaining.

- Food and or drinks are a bad idea unless this is a multi-hour or day-long planning session.

There you have it.

Seems simple because it is.

That being said, I would like to recommend a great book on meetings called *Mastering the Rockefeller Habits* by Verne Harnish. This book gives you all the info you will ever need to know about meetings.

Reason #5: Lack of Urgency

This may seem out of place in a Time Management section but it is actually right at home.

One of the biggest time sucks you have is your own lack of urgency.

I am not sure when or how it happened, but these days it seems that many people are just leisurely cruising through life with the, "I'll get to it when I get to it attitude." Sorry to pop your bubble, but you'll sing that tune all the way to the poor house. There is an expression that says, "Fortune favors the Bold."

Yes, it does. It also favors the speedy.

A gazelle on the Serengeti in Africa cannot afford to be slow and lazy. A gazelle is prey for the lions. You, my friend, will be the gazelle in business with an attitude that is anything less than urgent. You will, like a careless gazelle, be slaughtered.

The "truth" is that none of us know when our hourglass will run out. The "problem" is that many people think it never will. Oh, but it will. As I write this chapter, my mother-in-law, whom I love, is battling Alzheimer's. I cannot begin to tell you what a wicked disease it is and would not wish it on my worst enemy.

The torment she and my father-in-law are going through is heartbreaking. They both know that it's over. They also know that they unfortunately wasted much of the time that they did have. It's too late now.

Don't go to that place. You won't like it.

Don't fool yourself into thinking you have tomorrow. Maybe you do, maybe you don't.

What you have is today, that's it.

You need to develop a "grab life by the throat attitude" and operate as if there really is no tomorrow, because there may not be. I promise you that life will give you what you want, but there is a price. The price, however, for getting what you truly want is the best deal in town.

The price for sloth, you cannot afford.

Operate with urgency.

Reason #6: Email (See Phone and Internet)

Yes, another ball and chain keeping you from your pot of gold. Hopefully, you remember when we did not have email. Remember that? I would be willing to bet that you functioned quite well. This is nothing more than another method of someone wanting to take you to his or her product or service. On the personal side, it is not much different than someone walking into your office for that "Just five minutes" deal.

Email has its place.

But, just like most drugs it is, more often than not, abused. You **do not** need to check your email every five minutes. As I said earlier, no offense, you are not that important and anything of *real* importance you will find out about sooner or later.

Back off.

I actually know a few *very* rich and *very* successful individuals who refuse to use email.

They understand that their fortunes were made before the advent of email and while it may be a convenience, it is not a necessity to operating your business. As in the case with cell phones, as a society, we have become conditioned to keeping the umbilical cord plugged in.

Yes, *conditioned*!

Keep the email-checking to once or twice a day, not 100 times a day. I promise, you will survive. If you're concerned that customers will be upset, simply inform them that you only check your emails once a day.

TRAIN YOUR CUSTOMERS AND DISCIPLINE

YOURSELF

And as far as you being the one blasting people with email?

NEWS FLASH!

Most emails are deleted without being read. If you really want someone's attention, nothing beats a great direct mail piece. Remember that, direct mail? Yeah, it's the next big thing that never left.

Try it sometime. Or go to the direct mail section right now.

Reason #7: All Social Media

More and more I am beginning to feel like I am in the land of the walking dead. Social Media has got to be the biggest waste of time ever to see the light of day. Even Rubik's Cube makes you think. Not social media. If anything, it dumbs you down *fast.* I am not going to waste any time going off on a personal rant against this trash but if I did, it would be a good one. For sure I would offend lots of Face Bookers and Tweeters. I will save that fun for another day.

From a productivity standpoint, sorry, I just don't see it.

I very strongly believe that the value placed on social media as a business vehicle, is **grossly** overvalued. As with some of the other things mentioned, I am not saying that there is no place for it, but I am saying the actual level of value it brings to you personally and on the business front is very, very low. From a productivity standpoint . . . *ZERO.* I'm sure that there are many who would disagree with me on this, probably the same people telling us what they had to eat last night or what they did five minutes ago, but . . .

When discussing employees, I frequently used the terms, Measure and Manage. It is no different here.

If you can measure something, you can determine the probable outcomes. I have worked with many business owners who have bought into the social media business and services marketing B.S. and gave it a real shot. I mean they really worked diligently, with a good plan and budget. Nothing half-assed. They also closely monitored the progress. To a person, their determination was that social media was a complete waste of time and money as a sole or main advertising vehicle. Every so-called marketing wiz out there wants to sell you on the power of social media for your biz.

I'll tell you what. Have them pay for it and see how enthused they are.

Reason #8: Television

Let's say you go out and buy yourself a nice big ole' top of the line 900" plasma television that is bound to impress not only the entire neighborhood but even the good Lord himself. As this is now your pride and joy, you can't wait to have folks over to show them this Eighth Wonder of the World. After all the oohs and aahs, someone says, "Wow, how much did that cost?" You proudly say, "I paid $4,300.00 for that baby."

(I'm making these numbers up gang, work with me.)

So, here is the real question.

Is that *really* how much it cost? Yes, that may be how much you paid, but is that what it cost?

Are you following me?

Sure, you paid $4,300.00, which was the *price*. The cost, however, is *far* more.

Why?

Well my guess is that unfortunately you may be spending far too much time in front of your new pride and joy. This is time that you will never get back and time that could have and *should* have been spent on more productive activities.

When you add up the time *lost* watching television and equate that into dollars, you will see that you may have overpaid just a bit.

Hey, I am not saying that you should never watch TV. I enjoy watching the ball games just like everyone else.

What I am saying is that most people spend an average of three hours a day watching television. That is twenty-one hours a week. It is a whopping 1,092 hours a year. If you valued your time at only $20.00 an hour, that is $21,840.00 a year out of your pocket. You may scoff and say. "Well, that's not a lot of money."

Really?

I have a feeling if I walked up to you with a check for twenty grand in my hand you would not be scoffing.

Listen, just be smart. Don't get sucked into the mass brain-washing. If you want to spend a few hours a week in front of the set, fine, have at it. Just remember though, it comes with a price, and that price is *not* what you paid for the thing.

I suppose that I could continue to list any number of activities that are time-wasters, but those are the main ones. I'm sure by now you've gotten the point. When you have clearly defined objectives that need to be accomplished, you simply eliminate anything that does not add to getting said tasks done.

I know that sounds very simple.

Why?

Because it IS!

Here, let's make it even easier by quoting Nike, "JUST DO IT."

Where and When to Work

When you are talking about maximum productivity, it is super important to operate in conditions that are favorable to you. The two main conditions I am talking about are:

- *Time*

- *Surroundings*

Let's start with time.

As I am sure you can see, there are a number of recurring themes in this book. One of them is how people have been conditioned to fit someone else's agenda.

From a *time* standpoint, we have been conditioned to wake at certain times, work during certain times, eat during certain times, and so on.

This is a mistake.

Time can be very flexible in many cases. Most entrepreneurs and business owners have certain "peak" times of the day when they are most effective. Before I discovered this I used to think that there was something wrong with me.

I would be *very* productive early in the morning and mid-morning. And then between, one and three in the afternoon I would just be useless and not very motivated. Right after three in the afternoon, I'm back on it. It has been very useful to me to understand that you need not conform to so-called, "traditional work hours."

Determine Your Peak Working Times

Where you are putting in your time is a very important component to time management. It may not seem to be on the surface, but if you look closer, you will find that most people do not operate to their full potential when the environment is less than stellar. In other words . . . it sucks.

When at all possible, put yourself in a position to do your work in an environment that inspires you. For instance, as I write this chapter I am sitting on the back patio of my Scottsdale, Arizona home. I live in the desert, which is beautiful enough, but I have a million dollar view of the mountains too. It is very easy to be inspired to bang out work in an environment like this. The other day, I was at the world's greatest bar, called Greasewood Flat. You really need to see this place and people literally come from all over the world to visit. I go there some afternoons, grab a coffee, and write or do whatever else I need to get done that day. Again, *very* easy to be productive in a good environment.

Should you be in a position to work wherever you want, I strongly recommend you find a place where you can not only be less stressed, but more productive.

If you happen to be landlocked and cannot really work remotely, be sure to make the space you have a creative, inspiring environment. In my old home in Pittsburgh, I had my office set up in such a manner that you could not help but be inspired, i.e. more productive. My bookshelves had hundreds of books. (I read them all by the way.) Pictures of Carnegie, Lincoln, and Henry Ford adorned my walls. I had awards I had won and testimonial letters from clients. I actually felt smarter just walking into the room.

The point is that no matter where you are you can create a space that will help you be more inspired. And yes, that has a lot to do with time management.

Some Additional Thoughts

- Be very careful of associations. I will cover this later but just beware of the potential productivity suck this can be. People, employees, etc.

- When you can, work from home. The commute time is a bit more favorable.

- Say NO more often. Many people are people pleasers and being such feel bad about telling someone no. Again, this is *YOUR* time being stripped away to fill someone else's agenda.

- Work non-stop when the time is right. As I said earlier, there will be times when you find yourself at peak activity. Sometimes however, you will find yourself in what is well known as "the ZONE" This is when you are "out of your mind" unstoppable. When you are in that space . . . keep going. When I am writing for example, sometimes I can only get out five or so pages before I am trailing off. Other times however, I can knock out fifty pages without batting an eye. When you're on a roll, keep rolling.

- Stop making excuses. Another one that may seem odd for time management but if you think about, how many people do you know, and maybe know *very* well, who spend hours complaining about anything and everything. Listen, life is not fair and there are no guarantees. Get over it. Create the world you want. Stop wasting time complaining about things you cannot control.

- Set deadlines. Deadlines are a wonderful creation, unless of course you are going to miss yours. Put yourself under the gun and set a deadline. When I set out to write this book I didn't say that I needed to write 300 pages in one day. What I did was say to myself that giving myself three months from start to finish. I then broke that down to daily and weekly tasks that needed to be completed. It is also helpful to put yourself on the hook with others as far as completion timelines.

- Delegate. As entrepreneurs we always feel we need to "do it all." Well, you don't and you shouldn't. The reality is that you will probably screw up most of it anyway. The Mastermind Principal from *Think and Grow Rich* by Napoleon Hill is probably the greatest success concept ever created. Other people's time, talent and money. Focus only on what you are the very best at and delegate the rest.

CHAPTER 7

Uh-Oh

As the old saying goes, sometimes "shit happens."

We don't want it to, but it does, in every business and to everyone. The reality in life and in business is that sometimes, things just don't work out.

What do you do when your business venture is not working out?

Unfortunately, the odds are stacked against many of you, especially if you are trying to feel your way through things, which, by the way, makes this book worth a million dollars to you if you're smart.

Let me break this down in order of procedure on what to do if you are in the danger zone so you're not flopping around like a fish out of water.

The first thing you need to do is to *accurately* assess the degree of the issue. Is it just day-to-day, pain-in-the-butt business issues or is it the stake through the heart?

Chicken Little

It is easy to panic and overreact when everything is on your head. You start to think that the world is coming to an end and you are going down with it. It's very easy to get caught up in that. That, however, is not going to be very productive. You won't think clearly and you may make rash decisions that make things worse.

Listen, the truth is that it's only money we are talking about here.

Money is VERY replaceable. Don't get overly rattled about minor issues.

So Number One is to assess.

If the issue is not a deathblow, take a step back and rationally look at what the issue is and what needs to be done to get rid of it. I'm assuming, of course, you really want to continue in business. I understand that this may be easier said than done when you're trying to meet payroll but it needs to be done nonetheless.

Look at the issue for what it *really* is and not the horror story you are probably creating in your head.

What IS the Problem?

If it is a cash flow issue, which is the case with many small business owners, determine exactly how deep that hole is. Remember, it is critical that you have "accurate thinking" on this. Actually, accurate thinking is one of the key principals in Napoleon Hill's *Think and Grow Rich*.

As the saying goes, "It is what it is."

Gather your key financial person and crunch numbers. If you are the sole financial guy, grab your accountant and some booze . . . just kidding about the booze. It is also very helpful to bring someone in who is not as emotionally involved as you, especially when it comes to money.

Dig deep and find out IF you can get out of the crisis and if so, how do you do it . . . step by step.

You would be amazed what a good plan can do as opposed to flying by the seat of your pants.

Yes, I'm talking to you.

Put together a plan. Can you negotiate any debts, get more sales, collect past due receivables, etc.? You really need to throw everything you've got against the wall and see what sticks. Depending on your type of business, sometimes you are only a few sales away from getting back on your feet. So don't panic, yet, and look at the real hard numbers.

Find the REAL Issue

Remember this saying, "Math doesn't lie, people do." The numbers will either work or they won't.

What if it is not a cash flow problem? Frankly, if it is not a cash flow problem, you really don't have what I consider a *major* problem, unless you are involved in criminal activity or a regulatory agency is breathing down your neck.

Death of your cash flow is really the only thing that can permanently kill your biz.

Maybe it's an employee issue? I hope I made my point on that subject but in case I didn't, go back and re-read.

If you got a bad one . . . GET RID OF IT.

Yes, I said IT.

I have zero respect for deliberately bad employees who take advantage of the good will and finances of business owners.

Regulatory issues? Guess what?

Big Brother *IS* watching and watching *VERY* closely.

This could be an issue. If you think that Government agencies and regulatory bodies are the good guys out to protect the unsuspecting public from the big bad wolf, no pun intended, you're wrong. Very wrong.

They, my friends, are some of if not *THE* dirtiest players in the game. And when you are dealing with bad guys the rulebook goes out the window, at least for them.

Just to give you an idea on how deep this goes, I have personally had a regulatory agency tell me that a *LEGAL AND BINDING CONTRACT*, written by attorneys, and signed of free will by an individual . . . *DOES NOT MATTER*.

As I said: if they want you, they make the rules.

I realize that I may be repeating some of this from the legal chapter but it surely does bear repeating. If you are in a situation where your business is up against the government and or a regulatory body, you *MUST* get very, very good representation. As much as I do not like to use attorneys, sometimes it is a must, and this is one of those times.

If this is a BBB (Better Business Bureau) issue or something of that nature, you can deal with it on your own. Anything else, bring in the big dogs. Whoever you bring in **MUST** be well versed in these issues. You need to remember the beast you are dealing with. They have no rules. Think I am kidding?

I have a very good friend by the name of Bill Bartmann who, at one point, was worth 1.1 **BILLION** dollars and was the twenty-fifth wealthiest person in the United States. The government, led by Attorney General John Ashcroft, came after him on trumped up charges of insider trading. He was facing over 200 years in prison!! He fought and he won, but they sent him into bankruptcy.

Over 3,000 people lost their jobs and he lost everything he had. The government sent him a letter of apology when they discovered his innocence.

Yeah, it's that serious.

On the flip side, Bill, who is one of the greatest entrepreneurial stories in history, had a comeback. Once again he is a multi-millionaire AND he and his company have been nominated for the Nobel Peace Prize in 2014.

Not too bad. Yes, there can be a comeback.

So, back to what to do if Big Brother is after you . . . get great counsel, and keep your mouth **SHUT**. It is **VERY** tempting to mouth off when you know you have done nothing wrong and are being attacked, but you need to keep a lid on it. Let you counsel deal with it, keep your head down and try to survive.

If, on the other hand, what you did was intentionally criminal in nature. You're on your own and I hope they get you. As a matter of fact, throw this book out; you're not anyone I want to be around.

Time to Sell

One more thing to consider if you are in deep water is selling your business.

You would be surprised how many people are out there that may be willing to buy potentially viable businesses. You may have some unseen assets that may be very valuable to someone else. A good customer list for example.

The point is you need to explore all options when in a hole.

So what if the biz cannot be saved? What if you have determined that there is no way out of the jam you're in? Well my friend, you will not be the first and surely will not be the last to bite the dust. I could fill two pages of legendary figures who have filed bankruptcy; some of whom have filed multiple times.

It ain't pretty, and it ain't painless, but it also ain't fatal or permanent.

Trust me, I know. I have had my share of financial wipeouts only to realize how easy it is to recover. If you need to file bankruptcy, get it done and get back on the horse.

As I said, it's only money, paper with dead presidents on it.

That's it.

There is lots of money out there just waiting for you to go and pick it up. This is not a **real** problem. Real problems are kids with cancer, or people starving, or any number of REAL problems.

Money is not one of them as long as you realize how easily replaceable it is.

So if you need to go down with the ship, go down. But as with any good captain, make sure you save as many people as you can before you go down. If you're going through a bankruptcy, some people are going to be hurt, just try your best to limit that number especially the "little" people. It's bad enough that you're in it, so keep the collateral damage to those who can least afford it to a minimum.

Bankruptcy is NOT Failure

On a personal note, I want you to understand that a financial wipeout does **NOT** define who you are as a person.

We all tend to feel like failures and losers when this kind of thing happens but that is not the case. Yes, the business venture failed. Maybe your decision-making along the way helped speed this up. That doesn't mean you are a failure as a person. It's only money and its only business.

Like I said, better people than you have gone down in flames. Own it, but don't take it personally.

So now what? You're on your back looking up at the curb.

Congratulations! Nowhere to go but up now.

Assuming of course that is your intention?

It is right?

IF you learned from your mistakes you are at a very big advantage to start again . . . with a clean slate for that matter. Also during this time, it is critical that you feed your head with quality personal development material. You will be going through some dark days so you need to have information that will help you view things from a more positive prospective.

As they say, "This too shall pass."

. . . What are you waiting for?

CHAPTER 8

People Are Talking About You

O h yes they are! The million-dollar question is, "What are they saying?" When you break down a business to its simplest form, it's about attracting, capturing, and retaining customers. Obviously you need a good product or service to do this, but there is one component that I will say right now, will make or break you.

And here it is . . . *CUSTOMER SERVICE*!

You see, the reality is that if you do not have happy customers, you will have no business. With our current economy, keep this in the forefront of your mind.

Years ago, before the birth of the Internet, although you shouldn't have, you could have operated a business without too much concern about a few unhappy customers. Business owners would get paid, the customer would be unhappy and the business owner would just say, "Next." Unless you were very ethical, there was no major concern about a backlash that could put you out of business.

Sooooo . . . here we are today . . . the Internet age . . . there are no secrets.

Following the above scenario today, that unhappy customer gets online and lets the world know what a horrible business owner you are and that your product or service sucks.

Too many of these and you are out of business.

I have seen it happen over and over.

Bad news spreads like wildfire on the Internet and if you take advantage of a customer, look out. We will be covering in a later chapter the damage the Internet can cause, but for now, let's talk about how to prevent that from happening.

Let's talk about something that can make you and your business **VERY** successful.

Let's talk about the secret weapon for any business . . .

RAVING FANS.

Yes, raving fans!

Customers who are so blown away by your product and service that they want to tell everyone and their brother.

This **can** be done.

As a matter of fact, your business survival depends on it. Your competition is too tough to have it any other way.

Unfortunately, **many** business owners put this on the back burner. They take the money and say, "Next." That may work temporarily, but eventually, it will be your downfall. You **MUST** put customer service at the forefront of your business. And not just because it's the **right** thing to do, but because it's the **smart** thing to do.

You should not be selling a product or service that you are not totally proud of and you should never have the attitude that you do not care about the complete satisfaction of the customer. And I mean *NEVER*.

Some of you may already have this down. This may be second nature to you. However, my experience is that most business owners get a failing grade when it comes to customer service.

You are in business, I am assuming, to make money. You need to manage this as math. Happy customers come back, and tell lots of people. Unhappy customers don't come back . . . and tell lots of people.

You do the math.

How do we create this "Raving Fan"? When I look at my experiences with customer service, I think of Zappos, which is widely known for their customer service. Zappos is the mega company they are *BECAUSE* of their customer service.

"But I'm not Zappos," you say. "I can't provide that level of service." Well, you're wrong. Remember the saying, "Little hinges swing big doors"?

You do not need to be a mega company to provide a *WOW* experience.

Beverly International is a bodybuilding supplement company based out of Cold Spring, Kentucky. They produce and sell bodybuilding supplements. I will go on record as saying that I believe they have the very best products in the world. I am, and have been, a long-time customer.

The key phrase there is, "long-time customer".

The question is why?

As great as their products are, that is only one part of the equation for their business success.

Remember, you have **product**.

And you have **service**.

Their products are the **BEST** . . . the service, is totally a **WOW** experience!

As a customer of Beverly for years, I am **STILL** blown away every time I place an order.

As a matter of fact, every time I either place an order or receive my order in the mail, if there is someone in the room with me, I will immediately brag about what just happened.

I am not an individual who is easily impressed, but I would personally put Beverly International up there with Zappos. If you were to speak with the owners, Roger or Sandy Riedinger for any more than a minute, you would know why their customer service is what it is. It is not a service with them, it is a culture. That is a very important distinction. They don't do it as a necessary component to business success; they do it because they genuinely **CARE** about the client. By the way, they call people clients, not customers.

They operate on a deeper level.

"O.K., Jim, that's great, they sound like super people. How and why does that apply to me and my business?"

It applies because their treatment of "clients" has created an **army** of raving fans! The people who use Beverly International products talk about it….**A LOT!** I found this to be fascinating as it is ultra-rare to see this level of excitement from clients or customers in any field. More often than not, the experience is so-so with the occasional pleasant surprise of very good service.

Dealing with Beverly International is far beyond that and their results prove it. With the exception of a few locations, Beverly products are not sold in stores. They are mail order, yet their business continues to thrive. They also do not spend tens of thousands advertising their products which, in the ultra-competitive supplement industry, is beyond impressive. Most companies crumble under the pressure of going up against competitors with million dollar-advertising budgets.

How do they pull it off?

Their "fans," their incredibly satisfied clients take care of that for them. Word of mouth advertising has always been the best advertising you can get and the Beverly army is out in full force.

This is what you need for your business, an army. It does not matter in any way shape of form what your business is. Even if you are a larger company with a big advertising budget, you must create and keep happy customers.

Your clients/customers hold the keys to the kingdom.

What follows is an extensive interview with Roger and Sandy Riedinger of Beverly International. What they don't know about customer service simply isn't worth knowing.

Interview with Roger & Sandy Riedinger of Beverly International and Jim Toner

JT: I am speaking today with Roger and Sandy Riedinger of Beverly International. Beverly International is the world's leader in body building supplement industry and I truly mean that when I say world leader because I have been a customer for years and it is not easy to keep me as a customer for that long. The products are absolutely amazing in an industry so full of subpar products. You guys are literally at the top of the mountain. But, that's not what I want to talk about today. As phenomenal the product line is, I think you have something much more valuable at Beverly and it is probably the key ingredient to its success for most business owners and it is also probably in this day and age, the number one reason companies go out of business and that is customer service. So I appreciate you two talking to me today, first of all. Welcome.

SR: Thank you. Great to be here.

JT: Let me start with this, as a customer and a consumer, I have been consistently blown away by the customer service of your company. It's not something, where I'm like "that was really nice", it is always a wow experience for me and it's a lot of little things you do. You guys have been in business for over thirty years, correct?

SR/RR: Yes.

JT: Where did this philosophy come from with the exceptional customer service? Back thirty years ago, there wasn't the internet, there wasn't the social media where people can really either tear you down or built you up. Back then a lot of companies got by, it was no big deal if you didn't have customer service but I'm guessing you started this way back then. Walk me through the process. Where did the philosophy come from and how did it all start?

SR: When we started our business, we looked at ourselves first, and it was like a self-development thing - trying to be the best you can be and just pulling out all the good things that you can from your inner self and then applying it to our business. We first looked at who we were and what we wanted to do for others, and then pretty much took that into our business. In the introduction you aid something you've pretty much been a customer of ours forever. We look at you as a client rather than just a customer, like you are under our care, like a doctor does his patient and we want to do everything that we can for you and as we started to build our business from the very beginning caring for others, doing the best of everything we could for others, best experience, empathy for them, that is pretty much where and how it started. We want to do the best for you in every way. Now it's Roger's turn.

RR: Along with what Sandy said, I think both of our backgrounds entered into our mindset and philosophy. Sandy's father owned a clothes store, sold men's clothes. She worked there from the time she was 11 or 12 and learned the importance of personal contact and not just satisfying, but more than satisfying the customer. Next she worked as a dental assistant for a few years and when you are in somebody's mouth like that, you should be very in tune with how they are feeling, so that is where the empathy comes in and I know that when we got married during that time, she would come home and talk about the good things in customer service that her employer did. Some of things he insisted on, I would call them policies were very good as far as treating the customer. Then, I come from the public education realm. I was a middle school teacher for 17 years and then a principal. That's all customer service, also. Especially in my middle school teaching, that empathy thing came through quite a bit because I had lower social economic students. You had to really have high expectations for them, yet be able to guide them rather than just expecting it was going to happen. So, we both had kind of that guiding, teaching background in our upbringing. I think it even goes back to our parents too, as far as her father had a store and mine had a car dealership.

JT: So then this was a core concept that you had within yourself when you were just starting. It wasn't like you started a business and said hey we better be good to the customers. It's something that was ingrained in you from the start?

RR: I think we had that value within us, but we didn't really recognize it. We both had empathy, which was a very important part of it. I don't think we really knew how to translate that necessarily into the business. So, yeah, our mind set was empathy and let's do the best we can for each individual person but we really didn't know how to do it. Other than take a lot of time with each client.

JT: Excellent. One of the things that to me that is so unique about what you do is the amount of things that you guys give away for free, that I consider to be incredibly valuable information: your whole discussion board, the eating programs that you have on your website. These are things that "fitness gurus" on the Internet charge lots of money for. You give these things away for free. I think that is an incredible philosophy, but I see a lot of business owners out there say well I can't give that away for free, how am I going to make money if I give things like that away for free? Can you touch on that a little bit?

SR: Roger and I met in his gym, and the fitness trainers there did all the training and all the work out programs for free. When I got out of college with my degree, we wanted to help people better their lives in the fitness and health industry. We did free nutrition and training consultations and all the information that we gave was free. The supplements were like a sideline that we knew we could sell. We just incorporated an optional supplement purchase into the nutritional and training programs that we offered for free. From the very, very beginning, all the information was free. Sure, we sat back and wondered, wow, should we really be doing this? Other people aren't doing this. I know we are different, but we just felt like it was the best thing to do. All of our seminars, all of our consulting, all of our body fat analysis, everything that we did, that we knew how to offer someone as a client being under our care, was a full service caring health and fitness type project for them which we did for free. And then what we sold and we got back as far as income came from the supplements.

RR: We did free consultations well into the evening, 11-midnight, after our regular jobs. And then as we went into this business more, we continued doing individual consultations for another 10 years or more. And we were able to compile those programs that we formulated and refine them and see which ones worked best for which particular clients and that is where this treasure drove of programs that we now have available came from. They have all been tested and refined in the real world with real people for more than a decade. So we really did a lot of that in our first formative years as a business. When the demand for individual consultations became impossible to keep up with, we started conducting free seminars. We would do three series' of eight-week seminars each year. So about 24 weeks of seminars per year, for a number of more years. All of this was part of customer service. I mean there was a slight sales aspect, but we weren't really hawking the product at all because really, we knew that No. 1, the relationship is the most important thing and No. 2 is that if you don't have your nutrition program, at least close to pretty good, you are not going to see near the results from the supplements. So it went hand in hand. The only difference was instead of trying to sell the nutrition program; we wanted to help people so we gave them the nutrition program free. It was amazing, Jim, we would start a Saturday morning at 8 and it was scheduled to go until about noon, but it would actually be about 2:30 before the last person went home. We have so many relationships with people who became clients 20 years ago or more and they still are today. They are not just our clients, but are still out there selling for us. Whether it be through referral or this is the best product or whatever. Zig Ziglar said, "You can get everything in life you want if you give enough people what they need."

SR: I'll also add that at the beginning when we started all this, we were really struggling ourselves monetarily. We didn't have any. We were in rough straights. When we looked at helping people, we knew empathetically that if "they were like us," they couldn't possibly afford to pay for each service we provided - the training, the diet, etc. There are people now who charge $1,000-$1,500 for a six week session or program. When we started there was no way our clients could afford that. So we just did what we did, we acted like we were them. What would we want to get if someone was helping us and then just did it that way.

JT: I'm sitting here listening to you and there is a big smile on my face because I am saying to myself, this is gold. This is such incredibly valuable information for a business owner. If there is a "secret" to success, you both just hit on it. You have created long-term relationships, and created raving fans. When I look at Beverly and the Beverly culture, I see raving fans and what a lot of people reading this probably don't know is that you don't even sell your product in stores. It is mail order. An average person will say, how do they succeed, they are not even in a store? And the answer, you just gave it. Because you have legions of raving fans that are out there just evangelizing your product and I know that because I do it myself. I told Roger yesterday, every time I hang up the phone placing an order, I run into my wife and say you are not going to believe what they just did, how they just talked to me. I'll get my order earlier than expected with little stickers, free VIP mailing. It's just the little things. Because of that all I find myself constantly plugging Beverly while I am at the gym. That the secret right there. So how did that tie in? How did that transform into success for your business, the fact that you don't sell in stores, you are strictly a mail order company, how do you measure your success businesswise? How has this culture you've created translated into business success because you are obviously a very thriving company.

SR: We are not big, like the major players in the industry. We have grown at a very controlled rate. Yes, there is a Beverly culture. We are in some stores, but not the major chain stores. We are in very select stores. They are mostly owned by people who often use Beverly products. They sell the products because they experienced the service and results *themselves and believe in the product. As far as how it's translated, I have used an ant colony as an analogy. There are all these worker ants out there, hundreds and hundreds of them. They are spread out throughout the U.S and they work non-stop spreading the Beverly culture because we are not in the major stores. These "worker ants" feel special and privy to a "best kept secret". They may not want to tell everyone at the gym about it, but they tell their best friends. They want to keep it close because it is a pride thing because it hasn't been saturated and over talked about, over advertised. It is something that is the best kept secret.*

RR: I think that one of the points that we teach our staff and should bring out is one of our business purposes is, "your job is to create and keep a customer". The emphasis is on the 'keep" rather than to create. We are letting our clients do a lot of the creation for us.

JT: That is brilliant business advice. So many business owners feel disadvantaged because they don't have a big marketing budget. Well, when you have a culture like yours, you don't need one because you've got the best advertising money can buy which is word of mouth. Not only are they telling people, they are enthusiastically telling people.

RR: Word of mouth needs to be emphasized even more nowadays because my goodness, with all the marketing, internet advertising, there is so much information out there that no one is paying attention to any of it. If you are watching a TV program, you are skipping through the commercials now. I forget the number, but there are millions of hits of advertising that each person experiences and would have to process each month, whereas word of mouth is right there in front of you. If a friend is telling you about a product or service you will probably get the message on the first attempt.

SR: It's where the power is.

JT What do you see as the average time span a customer that stays with Beverly and have you calculated the lifetime value of your customers?

RR: If they stay with Beverly, they are still with us. We have figures on lifetime value. We even calculate the one time buyer if there are four one-time buyers. A lot of times as a one-time buyer, they aren't sophisticated enough to realize the value they are getting yet. We would prefer someone who has had experience with other supplements, who has taken supplements before. They can tell the difference. Seriously, we had to go back, our accounting program blew up in 2009, so we have a pre-2009 and a post 2009 and we went back to 1999 when Sandy and I became the owners of Beverly International. We were distributors for Beverly International prior to that. It's still the same people. Today we just had lunch with a client from 1995, so many of them stay with us forever. But now again, I should qualify that, it's not like if they ordered just once. But if they ordered from us 3-4 times, in general, they will continue ordering. So I can't tell you 5 years or 7 years. I think we have a number somewhere where we averaged everyone, like the Gold Club people, OMG.

JT: I would be willing to bet that if someone did leave, the majority comes back because they won't find the quality product; they won't find the quality service.

RR: When they leave and come back they give us the greatest testimonials we ever get.

SR: We just got one yesterday who said the same exact thing.

JT: They tried something else and they realize?

SR: Right, she was on our program and she tried to get back in shape, she knew she was missing some items from our line. She said, "I know I was at my top physique best when I took these three things, can you refresh me on how to take it." That is a very common thing that we hear. It's pretty good. I like it when people say that.

JT I mentioned this to Roger again yesterday, that when I think of customer service, I think of Zappos and I think of Beverly. I know I sound like such a mark for you guys, but I'm just that blown away by what you do. We all know that with all the problems people have in business; employees tend to be at the top of that list. How do you translate your values of customer's service to your employees and how do you get people indoctrinated into that?

RR: It starts with our hiring process. We look for those traits in the person before they ever get employed here. I think that's No. 1.

SR: I was going to say we hire the right people with big hearts, with a caring attitude. We look for that as we interview them. We have hired a lot of people who we have relationships with, who we have known and by doing that some have been winners, some have not as far as work. But as far as how they treat clients, they have all been top notch. First and foremost they have the heart and they cared and they practiced empathy.

RR: From there we have a training program that we go through and more of it is on relationships than on actual skill development, because in general the people we hire already have some background with our supplement line. That is usually where we find the people to interview through our contacts. Then we have a training program and it is first on relationships and next it's on customer service and then it goes on down the line.

JT: It is scary to think how many business owners or entrepreneurs just don't get that philosophy. I don't remember who said it; I think it was Jeffrey Gitomer. He said, "If people like you, and they trust you, they will buy from you." You guys have that down pat. It is very interesting that you put relationship first. In the day and age we are in now, to me it seems relationships matter less and less. I see many business attitudes gravitate towards that. There seems to be a prevailing belief that with the technology available, customer service can take a back seat. I completely disagree. I think it is all going to blow up and I think the survivors and the businesses that are going to thrive are the ones that really have relationship-based businesses.

SR: I agree. It's the foundation.

JT: It's absolutely the foundation. What are some tips out there for business owners, simple, little things that you guys do that make a big difference? To me, when I get a package and I get that free VIP mailing discount, or something like that, what it shows me, as a customer is that you thought of me. That is what makes me a raving fan, other than the product. What are some of the other little things that you do that you make the experience, a wow experience for customers?

RR: One of the things I would say for business owners is to try to systemize customer service. For example, if it's a telephone business, exactly how would you answer the phone? We have one sheet that tells us exactly how to answer the phone. We don't call them policies; I guess we would call them procedures. One is "the anatomy of a telephone call". Basically, you smile before you answer the phone. Here is what you say. Make sure you know the customer's name. Make sure the customer knows your name. It is very basic, but all the important things get covered every single time. You mentioned Jeffrey Gitomer before. We have this forty question customer service quiz from Jeffrey Gitomer that we use. We do weekly meetings. We've been doing them since 2001 and there's a lot of personal development stuff because as Sandy started out the interview, we think our success is due to continued personal development as much as anything in us becoming better people and developing a successful business. We do that with our employees and we go over and over it, trying to make them better and better at primarily customer service.

SR: Communication. How to communicate? There are a lot of people who know how to talk. But, there's a difference in communicating.

RR: I would say, just make small incremental changes in your customer service and do it consistently. Once you make something part of your system, it has to be done consistently over time and you have to monitor it to make sure it is done and make another little improvement.

SR: We also look at our staff as a team. Everybody is doing the same type of giving back. How to answer questions, the proper things to say. Everyone should be doing and operating in the same fashion that way we don't have one person who is lagging behind. Everyone needs to be up to par, on the team and they are all giving back and doing the same thing.

JT: Here is a question that might be out of left field, because I can't imagine it happening very often. I'm dying to know how you deal with it. Do you ever get complaints, and if so, how do you handle them?

RR: We have a system for that too.

SR When anyone calls, it doesn't matter what it is, I can be a gym owner, and it can be a person that just didn't really like the product. We make a mistake; we ship somebody the wrong thing. They didn't get their product. We missed their order or item, whatever it is. The procedure is we answer the phone, we listen, we empathize, we always say we are sorry, because we are, and then we want to fix it. We want to fix it fast, fix it now. We want to make sure that person, no matter what the problem is, is happy when we get off the phone. We don't look at what it's going to cost us, how long it's going to take us to fix it, because we want to make them happy when they get off the phone. We will overnight a package if we made a big boo-boo. We always send an email saying we are very sorry. We have a system for that. We make amends. We do what is right. We make the client happy. Then we feel like we have succeeded. It is definitely a system.

RR: The first thing we do is apologize. We listen. We empathize. Then generally we ask them eventually what it would take for us to correct this problem. What would make you feel happy? In other words rather than us just having a policy that is how we handle this, we try to individualize so that the client is happy with the solution.

SR: We work with them, we don't say no.

RR: Then we send an email immediately after the conversation again acknowledging the error or the mistake and telling them we want to make it right for them. In order words, it is not just on the phone, but we also send a follow up.

SR: And we have a little card we print out that says we are really sorry for OUR MISTAKE and we sign it and we put it with their package.

RR: Like with the replacement product that we send out. We kind of have acknowledged it three times and we don't ever say it's your fault.

SR: Never. We take 100% responsibility.

JT: Even if it's their fault?

SR: Yes.

JT: That's awesome. You know it's very hard for someone to stay mad at you when you are killing them with kindness. This customer is really mad at us, just kill them with kindness. Unless they are a very unique person, eventually they are going to not be mad at you anymore because you are too nice to them. I love that you guys do that. You are really killing two birds with one stone. You are doing what you believe it, but you also are serving a purpose. You are taking care of a customer and making sure they are happy, so they are not out there saying nasty things about you.

SR: That's true.

JT: This has been absolutely golden. One of the biggest problems out there today is the Internet. Anyone can say anything about anybody. It can be a competitor making false accusations. It could be a dissatisfied customer. In this day and age you have to go above and beyond to keep people happy. As I said at the beginning, there are so many people that don't get that at all. They have no concept of that. Let me take your money right now, and who's next. Your philosophy is so different. It is strange saying that it is so different. It is the way it should be. But it is so different because nobody does it anymore. What advice would you like to leave with an existing business owner or a new business owner as far as creating raving fans and happy customers?

SR: Definitely setting up systems and make sure everyone on the team executes his or her part of the play. Keep at it with your team until it becomes part of their life, part of their DNA. Once you have this buy-in, mentally buying in, heart, soul and body to the process and how you operate, you and your team will begin to recognize other things. When you go out for dinner, shopping, buying a car, or at the bank you see how people communicate and you see how people treat you and how they operate. And because you have this in your DNA and you know, as you said, how it should be done, you can recognize how different you actually are. It takes time. When we talked about how we built this from the ground up, it takes time. We went slowly, we created this environment. Got the buy in with our team and then the operation and practice and it is not something they can just do overnight. They have to look at the big picture.

RR: From my perspective, along with what Sandy said. I think the core values, and we have three, No.1 integrity. We have 100% money back guarantee. That makes everything so easy if you follow it. When you asked about it or if there was a problem. We don't have a problem because our problem is to fix it for them. That isn't our problem that is our value. That is what we do. We don't have to think how much this is costing us because the No. 1 core value is integrity. No. 2 core value is customer v. client mindset. That is the customer is merely someone that buys once. The client is someone that buys more than once and who is under your care. And, our third core value is continuous improvement or could be called innovation. I like to look at it as single step, improve here. Make it a part of the system, and then add another part on, so you continually improve whether it is in product development or customer service. The other thing that I think stands out is we have an emphasis on "the secondary consequence". That's when you make a sale, what we are doing with that sale is we are intentionally trying to make sure we get the second sale. It is also true in all kinds of other things throughout life - you have to look beyond the initial consequence of whatever is coming up next.

JT: Great words of wisdom. Extremely valuable for anybody that will take it and run with it. So thank you very much. I'm just thrilled to be a customer.

RR: Well, thank you.

SR: Gosh, you have made our day. I've been smiling. It's been awesome. Thank you for inviting us into this. Really appreciate it.

Good us. Bad Customer Service

Now that you see how great customer service can drastically affect your bottom line in a positive way, let flip the coin and see how it can affect your bottom line in a **NEGATIVE** way.

Pay attention. This is the biggest mistake most entrepreneurs make.

As a real estate investor, I buy lots of properties. I also use real estate agents to buy these properties. When I buy properties, all I ask the agent to do is get me the listings, get me in the house, and get my offer in.

That's it.

I am a **dream** client.

A number of years back I was working with a particular agent who had been referred to me. We met. He appeared to be a go-getter so I decided to give him a shot.

Within eight months, I had bought twenty-seven properties from this guy.

Remember what I said about my requirements?

I am basically dropping money in this guy's lap. However, every time I had to call him he acted like it was a pain in the ass. Every time I needed an offer to be submitted on the weekend, it was a pain in the ass. Everything I asked him to do he made me feel like it was . . . right, you guessed it.

The straw that broke the camel's back was this. It was Christmas and I was receiving lots of very nice gifts from people who were very appreciative of the business I was sending them.

I also got something from my agent.

It was a Christmas card with **HIS BUSINESS CARDS** inside. He wanted me to pass them out.

Would you like to wager a guess as to what I did next? I did some quick math. He was making an average of $2,500 in commission on each deal I purchased.

$2,500 x 27 deals is $67,500 he made from me in eight months. Not only did he make me feel like I was imposing on him, he sends me a Christmas card with his business cards inside?

Are you kidding me?

I never contacted him again, which got his attention very quickly.

He called me and asked why I wasn't contacting him. I told him that I had moved on and that if he had to ask WHY, he would never understand anyway.

The Next Pieces of the Puzzle

Do you think I kept quiet about this?

No.

I told everyone.

I am the CEO of a real estate investment training company with thousands of clients. Guess who they ask for guidance on whom to use?

Right.

ME!

Do you think I recommended him? Nope. Not only did I not recommend him, I used him of an example of the type of realtor that they should *NEVER* use.

How much the long-term cost to him would have been is anyone's guess, but I assure you that it was enough money to buy him a new home and some very nice cars.

Remember, I was not asking him for anything other than to make my life a bit easier and don't get in my way or give me grief. In return I would make him lots of money. I also was not expecting a Christmas gift. But I didn't expect the slap in the face in the form of his Christmas card filled with business cards for me to pass out.

And now yet *ANOTHER* piece of the puzzle.

When you are dealing with a customer, the majority of the time, you have no idea who that person is. Take me for instance. I had a weekly real estate investment radio show on the biggest station in town and had lots of listeners. What if I had decided to tell the story I just told you, on the air?

He would be ruined. I didn't, but many people do.

These days everybody and their brother is a blogger.

Some good, some bad. However, many of these people really enjoy getting online and letting everyone know about their bad experiences.

Folks . . . that can destroy your business overnight.

I make it a point to treat everyone I deal with equally. I treat them like a friend. I learned a long time ago that you never know who you are talking to. I have done some big real estate deals with people who, at first glance, looked like they could have been homeless. Instead they were very wealthy investors from the Old Country who were not concerned with the way they looked.

They owned half the neighborhood.

You never know, so don't be stupid.

I strongly suggest you re-read the interview with Roger and Sandy from Beverly International and adopt their philosophy. I absolutely guarantee you that if you follow that philosophy; it will add money to your bottom line in a big way.

Should you choose not to behave in that manner, well then, good luck. The odds are not in your favor and neither is karma. Do the right thing and watch the money roll in.

Jimmy's Law

Great customer service is *NOT* an option!

CHAPTER 9

Your Marketing Sucks

As an entrepreneur and business owner, your job is to *AQUIRE* and *KEEP* customers who will pay you. Hopefully forever. I am absolutely stunned by the number of business owners who put their marketing, the most important part of the business, on the back burner. You may be reading this book for that very reason.

Let me be very blunt. If you have no customers, you have no business. Makes sense doesn't it? Then why are you not putting marketing in the forefront where it belongs?

I know why. It's because you're busy pissing on fires that's why. You're busy babysitting employees. You're busy doing everything but the one thing you should be doing.... marketing...your...business!

You may think that you are different and that your business is different. It is *NOT* different. Doctors, plumbers, attorneys, real estate investors etc., are *ALL* in the same business. Don't kid yourself.

You need to be **consistently** focused on bringing in a long line of long term, paying customers. **That** is how you get paid, which I assume is why you are in business.

Charitable organizations have this down pat. All they do is market for more customers to donate to the organization. This is **your** job too. Get it? Good.

So, how do you conduct your marketing?

Do you even have a plan, or is your plan to hang a shingle and hope loads of people just wander in? Believe it or not, that is what lots of business owners do.

They hope.

Sorry to break it to you but that is a very poor marketing plan as well as financial plan. You cannot hope. You need a strategic, creative marketing plan that is carefully thought out and applied and tweaked.

Marketing never ends.

You also need to grab people's attention, fast. We under a 24/7 bombardment of messages from sources with agendas designed to make us give them our money. This is what you are up against. You are competing with bigger organizations with bigger budgets so you better be good.

So the question is how do you compete?

Let's start with different, and not boring. How's that? Twenty years ago I was down in Myrtle Beach, South Carolina during the summer madhouse that attracts gazillions of people. There is also a **lot** of business competing for your dollar. Especially restaurants. As a matter of fact, there are so many restaurants that even though there are lots of visitors; they really have to fight to get the customer.

There was one place however that *always* had a very long line out front waiting to get in. The name of the place escapes me, but I can see their marketing as if it were yesterday.

Out in front of the restaurant, they had a white, 4 x 8 sheet of plywood on posts with the copy:

WORST FOOD IN TOWN – GUARANTEED –

DO NOT COME IN

Now, they obviously did not have the worst food in town. As a matter of fact, it was the best food I had the entire week. What they had, and what they understood was that they had competition, lots of it. And all of the competition was doing the *same thing.*

Same type of advertising, same message, blah, blah, blah . . . white noise.

What this place did was employ what is known as contrarian advertising. They basically went against the grain in order to grab the attention of the potential customer. They *cut through* the noise. Now once you get them, you need to deliver and deliver big, but that is a different topic.

So ask yourself? How is *your* marketing plan working? Do you know who your ideal customer is? Did it even occur to you that there would be an ideal customer for you? If not, I assure you that there is.

The most effective marketing effort for you to be focused on in your area is known as Niche Marketing. Niches are segments of the market place that can be drilled down into in order to find a very close match for your business.

These potential customers have very specific needs and wants.

Many business owners simply cast a wide net, and hope to bring in as many customers as possible. Now this strategy does work for many businesses. You place a TV ad and it is hopefully seen many hundreds of thousands of people, some of whom will fit what your target market is, and some who will not.

If you're advertising a hot new fitness club, odds are that the folks in the elder care home may not be interested. Still, there will be some in that viewing audience that will be interested in something like that. However, wouldn't it make more sense to be advertising on very specific stations and or areas of the market place where your potential customer is known to be found? In great numbers?

The answer is **YES**.

I think you will find that the more specific you become on who your ideal customer is, the easier it will be to find them in a cost effective manner.

If I am a music promoter and I am promoting an upcoming death metal festival, there is a very specific type of person I am looking to reach. Odds are, that potential customer will not listening to the local country radio station. They will not be listening to NPR radio. They will not be taking dance lessons at a local dance studio etc. No, they will most likely be listening to *genre specific RADIO stations*, or reading similar publications.

Do you see where I am going?

We are hunting.

Would you set out to go deep sea fishing in the desert? Sounds stupid right? Well, that very well may be your advertising. If your marketing is not working, there is one of two reasons.

Message and market. What are you saying, to whom, and where are you saying it?

You must remember this is your number one priority as a business owner; to attract and keep customers. Anything that does not do that is a waste of time and money. All you marketing efforts must be directed at your target market, and must be a direct response type of advertising.

Hopefully you know what I mean when I say direct response. That means, someone hears your ad, and they respond, fast.

That is where the money is.

Do not be fooled into thinking that you need to "brand" your business.

Oftentimes ego gets in the way of common sense when it comes to issues such as this. Branding your company, in my opinion, is a very big waste of time and money. Advertising sales reps will often push this on you as the path that should be taken. I recommend that you throw them out of your office should that occur.

Listen, you're not Coca Cola, forget about branding and concentrate on bringing in your ideal customer. You can worry about feeding your ego later once you're rolling in the dough. The reality of all advertising is that no matter what medium you choose to take, you need to compete and you need to be good. No way around it.

So if Step One is finding your ideal customer, Step Two would be where do you find them and what types of medium do you use?

In the past, I have extensively used and spent lots of money on the following advertising outlets.

Here are some thoughts to consider.

Television Advertising

Personally, I am not a very big fan of TV advertising. Bruce Springsteen sang in one of his songs, "57 channels and nothin' on." Right on Bruce, only now, there are 5,000 channels and there is *still* nothing on. Though I have made money with T.V. advertising in the past, I found it to be the least favorite and probably the path most business owners should not go down.

Here are my top three reasons why:

1. Cost

T.V. ads can be very expensive depending on the market and the run schedule you get. If you are in a major market place such as L.A. or New York, you better believe you will be paying a pretty penny to get on the air. Smaller markets will obviously be less expensive, but airtime is not the only expense you will be looking at.

2. Spot production

You need to have a spot created and produced in order for it to get on the air and that can entail a hefty price tag. Unless you are an exceptionally creative copywriter and producer, or have someone in house, you will need to hire an outside agency. Price will vary depending on where you are in the country and the type of spot that you will be doing but in most cases, you will be looking at thousands of dollars even before you get on the air. This is not something most small business owners can afford, especially if just starting out. Produce and hope is not a marketing strategy.

3. People don't WANT to hear your spot

I know that can bruise the ego a bit but it is a fact. You and your business are not the center of the universe. Other than during the Super Bowl, I cannot think of anytime that people are anxious to see a commercial. What happens more often than not is people either fast-forward through the commercials, turn down the volume, or DVR their way through the program. Either way, your message does not get heard. Money down the drain.

In my opinion, the ROI (Return on Investment) does not add up. You cannot afford, in this ultra-competitive marketplace, to hope and pray your advertising will work. TV is one medium that is just not that cost effective for most business owners.

Overall, although it may seem very tempting to go the infomercial route, doing it on a national level is a very bad idea for most. If you really believe you have the world's "next BIG thing" give it a shot locally and see how the response is. Smart business owners test and test.

If, and only if, you have a very good response on the local level, then you can carefully consider going further.

And I do mean *very* careful considering.

INFOMERCIALS

Please refer to the above quote from Bruce Springsteen . . . the one about "57 channels and nothin' on."

The prospect of infomercial advertising looks very appealing on the surface. There are a number of infomercials that have been on the air for years and you have undoubtedly seen some of them many times. You may have even bought the product that was being sold. And yes, some of them make mega-millions! No doubt.

However, the *VAST* majority fail, and fail big.

Yes, I was one of those who failed with my "next big thing" infomercial.

I am not here to pooh-pooh infomercials or stop you from doing one. What I *do* want to do is let you know that if you should decide to venture into this world you better put your big boy pants on.

Of all the advertising mediums, I personally consider this to have the most potential danger.

Many years ago, you would have had a much better chance of succeeding if this is the path you were going to take. Today, with the tech explosion and the number of ways people get their information, the odds are *not* in your favor. Here are my major issues with a business owner doing an infomercial. And remember, I have done this so I am not talking out of school.

#1 - Cost

For most small business owners and especially new business owners, doing an infomercial will be cost-prohibitive. Unless you really have money to burn, your money can be better spent. Between production costs, hiring writers, talent, and airtime you are looking at some major cash outlay.

Production of your infomercial can run from $200,000 to 1 million dollars. Yes, that much. Of course you can get someone to do a "cheepie" for $10,000 -$20,000 but that is what it is going to be . . . cheap.

If you are *serious* about going into this advertising medium, you can't go halfway.

Airtime will cost you anywhere from $25,000 - $100,000 or more just for the **TEST** phase. Yes, the **TEST** phase. This is not the entire national roll out. This is a segmented part of the country and stations that will be used to gauge response to your product. Once the national rollout is put in place, you can be looking at $100,000 and up each week.

#2 – Odds

Business is all about numbers. The numbers in the infomercial world are big both in the win and loss column. Only about 1 in 10 infomercials will succeed on any decent level. I do not like those odds. Especially with the costs involved.

#3 – Competition

Again . . . refer to Bruce Springsteen.

There is **WAY** too much noise out there for my comfort.

Everyone and their brother are competing for your attention and your money. Lots of them have much bigger budgets than you. I know that part of being a business owner is ego. It's cool to be "the guy," or "the girl." And the thought of being on TV with your product can be very seductive. I get it. But what you need to do is really take a hard look at the math. As a business owner, I would hope your goal, in addition to providing great products and services for your customers, is to put **MAXIMUM DOLLARS IN YOUR POCKET.**

Am I right?

Yes, I am right.

There are much safer and less expensive ways to attract customers and I suggest that you try those first. Now, it's not all gloom and doom. For those ambitious types out there who are willing to go for the big brass ring, here is some good news.

If you should choose to take the infomercial path, and you should hit, it very well may make you rich. When infomercials hit they usually hit big. I happen to know a few people who have had their infomercial hit big and yes, they are rich!

So it can happen.

Another upside is that if you are dealing with a much respected infomercial agency which, if you are getting into this, you better have one; they will review and offer advice on your infomercial. It is in their best interest for you to succeed and having professionals in the business looking over your shoulder can prove invaluable. This is no guarantee of success but it *is* something in the plus column.

Something you may want to consider if you are leaning toward the infomercial route is local or regional infomercials.

Currently there are about 10,000 or more local cable systems in the US offering plenty of opportunity to buy in your local area, even on a community-to-community basis. The major advantage to this is cost. Local airtime for infomercials is relatively inexpensive for the exposure that you can get, turning you into an instant local celebrity.

Radio Advertising

Radio advertising is a medium that I have been pretty fond of for some time. I have made *A LOT* of money by way of radio advertising. What I like about radio is that it is fairly easy to drill down pretty deep into who and where your customer is.

For instance, in one of my companies, a real estate investment-training firm, we knew that our ideal customer was male, 35-55 years of age. We knew that a fairly large percentage of them were self-employed and, we knew that the majority tended to lean politically conservative.

So, what did I do? I found the top stations in every city we went into that had *THAT* customer. Normally this was a talk radio format. We would advertise heavily on these stations, sometimes using a well-known national name such as Glenn Beck or Sean Hannity, and we would drive them to a *FREE* live seminar.

Our message was tailored to the personality types who listened to that type of format. Our ads would hit on things that we know appealed to the listener's mindset, such as, "Are you tired of working for a living, tired of sitting in traffic just to go to a job you hate, all to make your boss rich?"

Do you see how messages like that would hit home with someone of a conservative leaning or someone who had a sense of independence? We would run 30 or 60 second spots heavily during the morning and evening drive times and then run a bit lighter during the rest of the day and weekends.

Why would we pay more money to run on drive times? First of all, bigger audience. Secondly, and more importantly, they were a fairly captive audience, and, I knew what their mindset was when they were hearing the spot.

I *KNEW* that they were most likely sitting in traffic like the spot said. I *KNEW* that they probably hated their job. I was reinforcing the conversation they were having in their head. I had the right message, the right market, at the right time.

We were so good at this that we literally could predict our monthly income by the spend we made. Knowing your numbers like this is an absolute necessity for your business. As my favorite saying goes, "If you can't measure, you can't manage."

I have included an interview with one of the best media buyers I know. As a matter of fact, we made lots of money together. A very good media buyer can do the same for you, but they need to be *very good*.

The following is an interview I conducted with my friend Kathy Svilar of KMS advertising. Kathy and I made LOTS of money with our advertising strategies and if you are wise, you will pay VERY close attention to what is being said in this interview. As I re-read this interview, I was making mental notes of all the comments that I can only imagine are costing business owner's untold sums of money out of ignorance. Now, you will be well armed. Enjoy.

Interview with Kathy Svilar of KMS Advertising and Jim Toner

JT: We are talking today with Kathy Svilar of KMS Advertising and Kathy, you've been in the media business for how many years?

K: I have been buying media since 1984. That will be billboards, radio, television, and direct mail.

JT: What I want to do is give entrepreneurs and business owners a sense of what they are getting into with the world of advertising because it is something they have to get in to unless you happen to have one of those businesses where someone can just walk up to your door and walk in and say, "Here let me give you money." You are going to go into the world of advertising which we both know can be very expensive and can be very dangerous to your livelihood if you don't know what you are doing.

K: It is extremely costly. That's the bad thing about making a mistake buying media. A lot of other things you can make a mistake and can recover. But when you buy, when you incorrectly place your advertising dollars, it comes out of your pocket, totally out of your pocket.

JT: Right. I want to hit you with a bunch of questions so we are going to break this down into media, radio, and print.

Back to your background. You have been in this business for a long time, but you have also been on the other end of it. Not just the buyer, but you were a very well-known celebrity talent in the East Coast, so you actually got to see behind-the-scenes and how things were bought. You really know the inner workings, which everybody reading this needs to understand how important that is.

I will tell you right now one of the biggest dangers is saying, "OK, I know I have to advertise so I will talk to this sales rep," and you will get a sales rep from a radio station or television or whatever and you will automatically assume they are the experts and they have your best interests at heart. Well, unfortunately, that is not necessarily the case on either one of those points.

K: Right. The best thing to know Jim is just what you said. When a sales rep is calling on you they have a "budget to meet" and they are out pressing and they are going to tell you everything you want to hear. Many times they do know a lot about the media that they are representing.

Many times, they do not, which is what is really scary. But, they are going to press you to buy their particular product, whether it's a cable television network, whether it's a broadcast network or a particular radio station. And I think the small business owner has to look at everything before they make a decision. So, whatever your message is that you as a business owner are trying to get out, there has to be a medium and a budget that will get your message to the right person.

JT: Ok, let's stop right there. I just want to backtrack very quickly something you said at the very beginning. This is a very important note for people to highlight this in the book here. When you are talking with a sales rep, they are going to tell you what you want to hear, and as business owners, oftentimes we are looking for somebody to save us. "I'm trying to run this business. I'm working my butt off 24/7. I don't know anything about advertising. Save me."

And, so you kind of walk in and I don't want to sound derogatory, saying walk into their trap, but they will tell you what you want to hear. What you need to know is whether what they are telling you is beneficial for you. Don't just think a sales rep has got it going on and all they are doing is living, sleeping, and breathing your business. No, they are going to sell you an advertising package, so you need to know if that package is a fit for you.

K: We want to be sure Jim, as a note, that when a sales rep is giving you information about their particular media, it is true. What we would like people to do is to at least check and see another venue and compare the dollars to dollars. That's all.

JT: Ok, let's do that. Let's go on the assumption that as a business owner you are going to advertise. As I said earlier, again, if someone has a walk in business and you feel you don't need to advertise or you really don't need to advertise, then that's fine. But I'm going under the assumption that everyone reading this right now, needs to do some type of advertising. So, let's start with television.

Now depending on who's reading this book obviously will depend on how large of a scale they are going to do their advertising or whether they are going to do a local, or regional, or national budget.

Let's just start with the basics of television advertising. No matter what scale you are going to do on, there is always that foundation of certain things that you must know. Because it looks really easy. Hey, I'll just go out and throw out a television ad and I'm good. We know there is much, much more involved. Let's start with the basics, a small business entrepreneur, let me get my name out there, I'm going to go into television, what are we looking at?

K: The television industry has two different entities, or two separate components. One is cable and one is what you would consider broadcast.

Broadcast television would be the major networks and this would be NBC, CBS, ABC and FOX. FOX has become the fourth network. It is a big player and each of those particular networks has a tremendous television programming. FOX, for example, is younger. FOX is where you will find American Idol. FOX is where Gordon Ramsey does all of his cooking shows, Hell's Kitchen.

I'm going to take each one.

CBS, which is little bit older and is winning all of the network battles. CBS is top of the line.

ABC and NBC are all good, but CBS is the leader right now. Which is interesting. I don't know when the time comes that this book is published that could change. So, I think the best things to know for an entrepreneur is \ FOX is definitely a younger demographic than the big three.

The fifth, sixth and hundredth, are the cable network stations.

Here is the biggest, difference, the broadcast stations is where your local news is produced. So, if there were a tornado, if there is a flood, if there is a news interruption, it would be on one of the big three. When you are on the big three, you have instant credibility. People see you on TV, they know you are real. So, as a small business owner to make your company have instant credibility, television is the place to be, without a doubt. It's also to most expensive because you are seeing millions of people reached. When you go on the cable network, that's really golden for a small business because you can absolutely tailor your message to your neighborhood. For example, if you are a citywide company, you might want to consider broadcast because you want everyone within a 20-mile radius of your location. Let's say you are an auto dealership; people will travel from one side of town to the other side of town for a car deal. But if you are, let's say a specialty food store, or even a hardware store, a nail salon, a spa, your sphere of influence may be three to five miles so that has a big bearing on whether you should buy cable television or broadcast television.

JT Let's take that apart for just one second. This all ties into the Cardinal rule that all business owners need to know WHO their customer is, and what demographic they fall into.

K: Exactly. Demographic is age, income level, girl or boy, who are you, who do you need. Geographically is where you would decide whether you want to go with broadcast or with perhaps a cable station.

JT: Right, for instance if you have a luxury car dealership, you sold BMWs, Porsches, and things like that, you probably would not want to target your marketing at lower income parts of town. You've got to know, ok, if I am selling this widget this is who buys my widget and where is that person? Where are they located? So you can't just throw things out there and hope they stick.

K: And, see here is what everyone says, I am an ad agency. I'll say to the client, who is your client? Oh everybody. And I say, "No. It can't be everybody." Now a grocery store could be everybody. But, high-end grocery stores, then you switch it off. Most of the time and with a high end product, it's younger, because honestly the grandmas don't buy high-end stuff. Pretty much, it's a younger audience. And, it's in specific zip codes that you can do with direct mail. So if you are a luxury car dealer, you may want broadcast television because it gets to everyone. They will drive twenty miles to get from one side of two to the other side because the BMW dealer is good. But, let's day you are dentist, or again, I use that nail salon and spa. Those people will need to advertise. You have to then perhaps go with a cable station and just buy your zone or your zip. Then you decide, all right, I'm going to buy my zone, but what station? With cable, there are 166. That's splinters up, totally divides the pie. Ok, you are getting your neighborhood, but what station do you want?

If you are a young nail salon, targeting females, maybe you want to be on Bravo. Bravo has stronger women, is a little bit younger and it has a high-income level. Their average income is $63,000.

If you were a guy, let's say that you have a bar or a night club or even an auto dealership, you may want to go on CNN in your neighborhood which that average income is over $100,000, on CNN.

Not only do you have to determine what neighborhood, you have to determine what age, female or male and then the income level plays a big part.

JT: You had mentioned you could do CNN in your local market, which I'm sure a lot of business owners may not be aware of. Most people think of a station like CNN as strictly national. However you could actually target that to your specific area, but you get the massive benefit of saying we are on CNN. So what this does is allow you to reach the right person, and gain enormous credibility with your customer because you are being seen on CNN, and you pay only local rates as opposed to national rates.

K: That's correct. You are paying for 30 sec cable spots, and depending on the station, the rates will vary. A thirty second spot is what I would recommend when a company starts out so that people would know who you are, and you have to stay the course at least six months. People do not have a long attention span. So they switch through commercials quickly. They might see the tail end of your commercial one-day and they might see the beginning of your commercial another day because they switched the channels and their mind is on what they are making for dinner. Consistency is the key. One shot, one week is not going to do it.

JT: So with the consistency, comes the budget. What kind of budget can someone expect to set aside for TV advertising?

K: With small business there is usually not enough budget. A media sales rep will say to you, "For $1,200 for the month we can do x, y and z for you." Now $1200, I would spend that in three days on broadcast television because my commercials are $300 apiece. On cable, you can get a lot of spots for $1,200, but you have to stay on for three to six months. So it's not $1,000, its $6,000. So when you compare $6,000 to something else, that's why the reps aren't exactly telling you the whole story.

JT: For the average small business owner out there, if they don't have what x amount, they should not even bother with TV. What's the amount?

K If you don't have $5,000 to $10,000 to spend for two months, don't even think about television. I do have some clients who spend $20,000 for two weeks and get extremely good results, but these people have been on the air for three to four years.

Don't let a rep convince you that $1,200 would make a dent. It won't.

JT: Now people need to understand that these are not the only costs associated with TV advertising, let's talk about production of these commercials.

K: In today's world the TV station will have a "deal" and the production will be included. Every television station has a creative department so they will wrap it in a package for you. But again, we are at $5,000 to $10,000 level for you to get free production. If you are doing cable television, most cable systems no longer have creative departments, but they have outside vendors. You can get a commercial produced for as low as $1,000, of 30-second television. My experience is between $2,500 and $5,000 is a quality piece that you would be very proud of, and you could use on your website, on your email campaign, on YouTube. So, that's a tough one for small business. $1,000 is what you are going to pay generally.

JT: Another potential killer for the uninformed is not only the look but the content of that commercial. Your commercial is your sales pitch and if you don't have a quality script, you might as well flush your money down the toilet. So the as a small business owner the question you've got to ask is, are you capable of writing quality content that will bring a customer in, and if you are not, where are you going to find that person and what are they going to charge? That number can get very high. Very good copy writers can charge upwards of $50,000 depending on the project so getting quality content is not cheap, and you can't just leave it in the hands of production and say, "Here write me a commercial."

K: Exactly. However, being the business owner and knowing your business as well as you do will allow you to "direct" anyone you may need to hire to produce copy for you which will save lots of money.

JT: So, that's a wrap up television in a nice neat little box. Know your customer, your product, and the message that you want your customer to hear. We also have to have a budget that will allow us to run for at least three months.

K: Yeah, I say three months. That is good exposure.

JT: So then the budget we also want to look at is, again, three months, and $5,000 - $10,000 minimum per month depending on where you are in the country.

K: Exactly.

JT: So, the take home is that if you don't have the budget, you need to find a way to get it, or you need to find another way to get customers because if you don't do it right, then you are just flushing the money down the drain.

K: Exactly. If I could add one thing from when you just said, you have to get it, when you are, let's say a grocery store, or a specialty food store, you can tap into your vendors and let them piggyback on your thirty second commercial. You can move to 15-second commercials and maybe have two vendors in a 30 second wrap around for you. So getting the money from people, who you buy from, your vendors, is a great way to come up with an advertising budget. Many vendors have money. It is called co-op or cooperative advertising and many, many vendors have that kind of budget available. You just have to get in line and do the best job in getting it for you.

JT: Before we move on, I want to say how important your credibility or your PERCEIEVED credibility is. I'm going to say a quote, now this may sound derogatory but there is a large kernel of truth to it and it was

PT Barnum, perhaps the greatest marketer in the history of the world who said, "Never underestimate the ignorance of the general public." What he meant was people believe what they want to believe. And when they see you have a commercial running consistently, whether you have a good product or not, unfortunately, people will believe it. "I saw that person on TV. It must be real. I've got to call them." As a small business owner, your business does not exist without customers... period. You've got to get those customers. When you are on television, it is instant credibility. It would be wise for you to re-read this paragraph again, and REALLY "get" what I am saying.

K: I want to add one more thing on television, we talked about demographics because women are a little bit easier to find because in the daytime there are all daytime programs for women. But, men are really easy to find because of sports. And, so many sports and broadcast on cable. So ESPN and the various local sports entities on your cable systems, whether it's your local college football team, whether it's basketball, whether it's the baseball, the major league baseball, those games are usually on a cable station near you. If you are a company that goes to men, sports broadcasting in a great way to reach them. There is even a golf channel. So men are a little bit easier to find on television if you just target sports.

And one more thing Jim, regarding what a sales rep may present. You need see from your rep not just a number, say $5,000. You need to see how many spots, where they are going to be placed, and the frequency. Now people will sell you a thing called a rotator. And a rotator spot in any of the mediums are kind of leftover. They are going to put you in wherever you are going to fit. Usually the price on a rotator spot is real low so you may think, "Holy smokes, I am really getting a great deal." If you can stay three to six months, go ahead and do rotator, but if you have a point of sale, a direct sale that you need this month, a rotator spot is like a general wherever it's going to fit, it will fit. So, I think that is *what the person has to ask, where is the spot going to be? How many times will people see it?*

JT: Let's talk about radio.

Radio is always been a favorite of mine. I've made a lot of money through radio. Radio is another medium that business must clearly understand how and when to use. I personally feel that radio has some big advantages attached to it.

K: With radio, you can have a smaller budget because a spot could be from $50 to $600 depending on what station. But, you are able to get better frequency on radio because there are so many of them. It's like the cable stations. With the broadcast TV, there are only four. With cable TV, there are 166. With radio, in a major market, there are probably 50 stations, and maybe 15 of them are top tier.

Frequency is how many times an ear hears your message or an eyeball views your message.

JT: That frequency you are talking about, you mentioned the number three. So whether it is television or radio, some will have to either see or hear your message at least three times before they take any type of action.

K: At least three times before they even think you are real. Actually, I prefer five because in today's world we are bombarded more than we were ten years ago by images all the time and we really tune out. So, that's why three to five times would be a minimum on a media buy.

JT: We are going to look at a frequency then minimum three, preferably five.

K: That's correct. With radio again demographics is super important. If you are a male, we have specific sports talk, the broadcasting of the actual games in various cities, so men are relatively easy. We go sports all the way. Women it's one of those deals where, who's your client?

Everybody! We want everybody. If you are a grocery store, maybe, but if you are a hair salon, you want women. Do you do higher end products? Then you want women that are working, more affluent and radio stations are very different. Teeny boppers, kids, there are stations that are just geared for just teens. If you are prom dresses, if you are Abercrombie Fitch, if you are a fashion entity, if you are music, if you are skateboarding, if you are rollerblading, you can find your niche. The radio is great for niche marketing.

JT: The most important thing is, just like TV, who is your customer? Because like you said Kathy, there are so many different radio stations and different people listen to different stations. For instance someone who is listening to country music may not be interested in a luxury car dealer. They may be interested in a car dealer that sells pickup trucks or something like that.

I told a story about our business. How we knew, who our customer was and we knew where to find them. Our customer was more of a conservative bent, generally males, and a lot of them, self-employed. A lot of them listen to talk radio, so we knew exactly where to go to find our customer. But when you veer off from that and try to go to other stations where that person wasn't, the results weren't the same.

K: Right, and just along those lines, when you have women and there are six stations that gear to women, you have to then go to the age demographic. Because music choices are very, very specific to age. Very specific.

If you have a senior housing or AARP couponing or early bird specials at your restaurant, then you are going to want a station that plays big band music and is very simple to find for seniors. But if you are a senior care center and you want the baby boomer who are making selections for their parents who are elderly, then you might want to go to a 60's, 70's kind of oldies station. If you want general women that are 25-54, then you are going to go to a top 40 with disc jockeys or airtime people, air personalities that are that kind of age group. We identify with our radio station in a great way, more than television. We listen on a daily basis morning drive. Morning drive, by the way, is the heaviest listened to radio because of traffic jams. We listen to the same station. We get to know the personalities on the air and we identify with that music and those people. It is gender specific and it is demographically specifically because income level. So what you have to do is know who you want.

JT: Let's talk about spot length for a minute.

K: Again, if you want frequency, which we do, you can buy a shorter time period. You could buy 30-second spots on the radio to get your name out there. If you have a specific sale going on and you need that frequency, for example, "Come in this weekend, we are having an all clad, kitchen product sale, 3-days only," we are going to do 15-second spots and we are going to bang them out there and we are going to hit a six frequency, and we are going to hit people who have money, boom. We got it.

If you want to campaign your new business and you need to explain who it is that you are and what you do, you are going to need a little bit longer time. 60-second commercials on the radio are unheard of pretty much anymore. They've moved to 30s and 15s. The radio stations are cramming in as much as they can to make as much money as they can. So the reps are going to sell you 15s and 30s. You are only going to want 60s if you have a bigger story to tell.

JT: That's all we really used to do were 60s because I had a story to tell. We were in the real estate investment training industry and had a story to tell and 15 and 30 seconds weren't enough to do it. But the 60s worked extremely well. But you are right; stations are trying to get you to do the 30s, which is a little more difficult to tell your story in 30 second.

K: Right, if you are not a known entity or if you are not selling something that is not known, if your product is unfamiliar to your audience, you have to have a longer format and that's where we go into half hour blocked programming, hour blocked programming which is hard to buy, but extremely successful.

Jim, this is a really important thing. The story to tell that you need 60 seconds, nobody sells longer than 60 seconds. You could buy two 60 seconds and back them up, it's called bookended. It could be at that top of the spot break and the bottom of the spot break. You could do two commercials. If you are going to have a product like a kitchen store we just did, we did 15 seconds, we were selling a product called All Clad and everyone listens to it, knows it. We bought a high-end female audience and we did 15 seconds and we blasted them. We bought lots and lots of spots for 3 days, that's it. Three days. We would never recommend 3 days if it wasn't something people desperately needed and knew about. The duration of the spot is in direct proportion of how much people already know.

JT: Let's talk about budgeting for spots. What should be a proper run? I know you said you just did a three-day, but it really depends on what you are promoting. We promoted a lot of seminars so we would do a 10-day run on spots. What about someone who is just promoting his or her day-to-day business?

K: Most of the time, people go on the radio for a direct sale. They have an event, they have a specific sale. This is truck month. The image thing, if you are going to doing image commercials, then you can spread them out, maybe do one week, do Monday, Tuesday, Wednesday. The next week, do Monday, Tuesday, and Wednesday. Then the last two weeks of the month, do a Thursday, Friday.

Only buy weekends, ONLY buy weekends if it's not direct sales, unless you are having an event that Saturday and that Sunday, you can blast it Thursday, Friday. Then that Saturday Sunday weekend listenership, people are on their boats, on picnics. It's not the same as that Monday through Friday. Monday through Friday is prime time for radio.

JT: Business owners should be looking for prime time radio, frequencies of minimum of three up to five probably 30-seconds or 60 if they can get them, with a run of Mon-Fri.

K: Yes. When a sales rep is sitting down with you, they are going to give you a package. You are going to have to compare that with at least one other station. Never buy without checking the competitor. Never buy radio without checking the competitor. That's crucial. That means you have to take the time up front to do your homework.

JT: When you say the competitor, you mean other stations.

K: Yes. And see what kind of deals they are going to offer. It is a very competitive market out there. The radio stations definitely cut deals. Definitely.

JT: One other thing to point out is you mentioned people that use radio for branding. I will tell you right now, I think it's a very bad idea, unless, it is free. Your goal is to get customers in the door and makes sales. You can worry about branding yourself when you are much bigger. If you are not getting on the radio to give a direct response message, I really think you are just throwing your money away.

K: Image is tough on radio. Unless you are going to . . . "Today's weather report sponsored by". But, you're right; unless it's free, take a pass.

JT: That is so important because business owners have egos and they get jazzed hearing themselves on the radio. But the idea of you being on the radio is to get a customer and feed your wallet, not your ego. So if you are going to do radio, it has to be a direct response message. "Hey, come buy my stuff."

K: Right, "Come buy my stuff," and then work a deal that this weather broadcast sponsored. That's the kind of freebies or extras that you should get from a radio rep. Radio reps have more play or a little bit more freedom to give away extras. Extras in the form of traffic sponsorships, *weather sponsorships, online billboards on the website, direct link to your website from their station website. So the freedom to get more freebies, through your radio rep is really good for radio. That is why you have to talk to two different people. You have to compare and you can't be afraid to say what else can you give me for my $3,000 or $5,000? You have to have the money. You cannot just do ten-days of radio and call it a day if they have never heard you ever before. If you want to begin a radio campaign and you want to do this traffic brought to you by, Joe's sports shop, great. But again, just be sure that it is a "throw in" as part of a package.*

JT: Now on the other hand, if for some reason you have a VERY big budget, preferably someone else's, and you want to spend some of that on getting your name out there....

K: Exactly. If you are brand new and you can do $5,000 the first week, go for it. But, Jim, as you know, you have more experience in radio than most small business owners in the country. You do, because you have done it in 11-12 different markets and you know what works and what doesn't work. Like you said, the branding can work, but it takes a long time and deep pockets.

JT: I think this is a good spot to give our readers a million dollar tip. Let's say you are a new business owner or an established business owner and you really need a bump in exposure and or credibility but you don't really have an unlimited budget to work with. There is a way and it is called "borrowed credibility" Things such as celebrity endorsements can sky rocket a business almost overnight. When we were breaking into new markets, I would use someone like Glenn Beck or Sean Hannity. I will tell you that were the best money I ever spent. Now, they have to believe in your product or service, but if they do, and you can get them, it can be BIG.

K: The celebrity endorsement can be a game changer, but you need to be sure your budget justifies using a celebrity endorser. You don't always need a BIG national name. You can get well known, local Radio DJs to do your spot. You can get well know local sports celebrities also. Now here are some things to remember. Does your celebrity endorser, who you are interested in, fit into your product? That's really important. It's probably not a good idea to have a male sports celebrity do lingerie endorsements you. If you have a product that a celebrity can try, the endorsement is a thousand times better.

JT: That is an enormous tip right there to get instant credibility and it all goes back to knowing your market, and your customer. The other thing is you have to make sure that celebrity endorser is somebody who is respected, liked, AND is aligned with your customer. The reason I did so well using Beck and Hannity is because they spoke to a conservative audience. Well, THAT is who my customer was. My message, coming from the right person, TO the right person created enormous success.

K: Right, that person has to believe in you. When your company had a national talk show host endorse us in 11 cities, he honestly believed in real estate as an investment vehicle. And, it came through loud and clear with his words. And we did phenomenal. There has to be a belief factor. And, that's the truth Jim. Glenn Beck, I've talked to his producers after we cut the spot and they'd say, man he wishes he could do it, he could invest with you. So, he really 100% believed in us.

JT: Newspaper advertising. What are your thoughts, do you still thinks it is still a viable advertising medium?

K: I think it is still viable, but mostly on a local level. Here is the reason. There is a saying about print, it goes like this. Print advertising is a destination while advertising in all other media is an interruption. So when you sit down to read the newspaper, you are sitting down to read the newspaper. It's your time; it's your choice. When you are listening to radio or watching television, the advertisings are interruptions. So, in that regard, print advertising is still viable. The issue is how many people are still buying newspapers, and what is the demo?

JT: That's a very good point. For a small local business owner, I think newspaper advertising is still alive and well with the right message and for the right price. So, walk us through the process of someone wanting to add newspaper to their advertising platform.

K: First of all, we don't give any kind of advertising a shot. We make an intelligent, informed decision and then we stay the course. I think that is one of the biggest things that small business does wrong. If I see an ad in a newspaper for someone, then I never see it again, I would have to try to remember their name, try to remember their website and then go and find them on the internet, most likely. So unless you are doing a time sensitive event, newspaper advertising should be an ongoing or at least a fairly long-term venture. I say that due to the affordability in local papers.

Step one: research what you are going to do between the valuable and viable mediums of radio, television, billboards, print, and direct mail. If you are going to select print, then find your local newspaper. If you live in a town that is a suburban section of a bigger city, most likely there is a small neighborhood paper. The example I am going to use is a neighborhood paper that goes to 16,000 homes. It's called the Times Express. It is in suburban Pittsburgh. My hair salon client, remember we talked about hair salon people might go 5 miles, but not go further. So we decided to advertising in the 5-mile radius around her shop. The best way to do that is the local newspaper, which is read like the bible. Here's why. It's the local politicians, local school board, and local sports. We make the decision we are going to go into the paper. The newspapers are very inexpensive because the advertisers are told that newspapers are dead, print is dead, so we were able to buy full page, color ads in this tabloid size newspaper. A tabloid is if you take a full sheet of newspaper, fold it in half and then turn the pages horizontally, that is called a tabloid section or tabloid format. So we buy a full-page ad for less than $200. If you are going to buy a ¼ page ad, it's $50, but *the full-page ad for $200, I convinced my client to do 2 a month. We take a beautiful picture of her interior. It's very spa like, with plants. We put a picture of her and a tip. So every week, or every other week, bimonthly, we are going to do her beautiful picture and a tip. So we want people to start to become aware that she is the expert and you are going to look for these tips. We had a lot of response the first time out because we put an offer. That's another thing we need. We need an offer. We had "Buy one, get one free" haircut. That was pretty good. A $35 value and we had four people come in. Well, that paid for the ad. The next time we do a tip, we have Kathy; she is beautiful, the gorgeous look of the spa and different kind of couponing, different kind of very, very classy looking photos and always an offer. We have been in the paper consistently now for one year. 6 months ago unbeknownst to us, her salon was voted the second most elegant, fabulous, spa salon in the eastern suburbs. We didn't know that we were even up for that kind of an award. It only comes from the consistency of that local paper. So I do like print.*

JT: That is a good story. So it pays off for a small business owner. Again, the key is consistency. We have that recurring theme here; the key is frequency and consistency in running your marketing.

K: You also get a better deal. If you say to the newspaper, a local paper, that is well read with local sports and your neighbor's kids' picture in it, that's what you want. The big metro papers that go to 1.2 million homes on a Sunday, you are going to pay $3,000, $5,000, $7,000 up to $17,000 for big sections in the metro paper. So, most small businesses think about 5 miles, 10 miles max around your location. Local newspaper is a winner in my book.

JT: Here is another great strategy that we kind of touched on it with the television. You can also advertise in the newspapers regionally in larger newspapers, such as USA Today. People assume that because USA Today is a national newspaper, you can only advertise nationally, but that is not the case. You can also advertise regionally. So, if you are looking for the credibility factor and you've got the budget, and it's a very well read paper, you can market your business with, "as seen in USA Today," and you can have copies of your ad included in your marketing literature. It is a very powerful thing. Again, when the average person sees something like that, they equate that to, "Wow, that must be a real company, it must be big time, because they are in the USA Today." That whole regional thing offers big potential.

K: Yes, that goes to both image and branding which when combined with a powerful call to action for a direct sale, this is a very powerful strategy. One of the other good things about print is that it's there whenever the person wants to read it. And magazines are often read by many people. Think of the magazines on airplanes or in doctors' offices. A newspaper comes into the home so you are counted as one, but most times, more than one person reads that paper, and, often times the paper is left around for a while or the ads are cut out so you have a better shelf life as opposed to radio or television, where people may not have the time to write down your message.

K: Jim, if you don't mind, I would like to touch on the power of the publicity that can be gained by doing something for others, which is what you did with the "Home for the Holidays."

JT: Sure, great story and a great lesson.

K: In 2005 when the war in Iraq was still popular, when our soldiers from our country fighting in Iraq, Jim's real estate investment company was booming, and Jim had a plethora of love for the veterans and simply wanted to use the skills he had as a real estate investor to make a big difference in the life of a veteran. So, he decided to give away one of his homes. So, we a contest where people wrote in to tell us why they would want to have a home for their service man or woman. The difficulty was two-fold. Initially, to promote the event to get the entries. In that situation, it was so unusual. What? You are giving a home away for free, no strings attached? It was a very intriguing and interesting story so the newspapers and the radio stations and sports talk specifically, brought us on to talk about it. The impact all of the publicity had on the company was incredible. We didn't do the home giveaway for publicity however; we did the home give away, to honor the men and women who were fighting for our Country. But, little did we know that a snowball was just starting. Not only did we get full page ads in every metro paper because of the generosity and how unusual this was, a free home, the day that we gave the home away, we flew the woman from Atlanta, Georgia, who had entered her brother, flew her into Pittsburgh and we gave her the keys to the home a week before Christmas. Imagine our shock when we got to the property and found four television stations, and one radio station parked in front with their trucks, and their big satellites. And then came CNN. We sent the information to the national news because it was just so unusual. Again, as a small business when you do something great, it could be viewed as really great by the rest of the world. So be sure you tell. When CNN showed up and broadcasted live our event, we were flabbergasted. It got better. Not only did CNN cover the house giveaway, but also they set up a live feed with the recipient who was still in Bagdad. So Jim was able to be on a television set in Pittsburgh PA and the exact moment that the satellite beamed up to the stratosphere from Pittsburgh it beamed down into Bagdad and we had a live feed with the young man that was receiving this home. So the publicity and the good feels, the good vibes, the good PR that came from a simple idea from the heart of one man provided us an impetus for two more years we used this to promote ourselves. So publicity and public relations if done properly, if done with the right heart attitude is invaluable. You simply cannot buy that type of good exposure.

JT: *Here is an important lesson about that too. I totally agree with you. There are too many people that do things to just try to get publicity. They don't do it from the heart, which I think is a big mistake. You have to do it for the right reasons. That being said, if you are doing it for the right reasons, you should absolutely try to get as much bang for your buck as possible. One of the ways we did that was we strategically timed this so it would happen about 8-9 days before Christmas. The reason for that is that is a slow news period and the media is looking for stories and looking for feel good stories. This was as feel good as you can get, which is why they were all over it. If you are going to do it, you need to do it for the right reasons, but do it in a smart business manner also. Time it out the right way. Do what you can to get the most publicity that you can. It worked great for us.*

My next interview is with another radio advertising rock star, Missy Wilson of Be Real Management. Missy is a Block Programming exert. Don't know what block programming is yet? You will, and it will be a pot of gold.

Interview with Missy Wilson of Be Real Management and Marketing and Jim Toner

JT: I'm here today with Missy Wilson, owner of Be Real Management & Marketing and I want to talk a little bit today about the Holy Grail for a lot of biz owners, what we call "Block Programming." Missy, take it from there. What is Block Programming?

MW: Block Programming, otherwise known as long-form programming on radio stations. It is a block of time that some radio stations offer for sale to business owners. Usually it is sold in a 30-minute block or a 60-minute block of time or longer. What it does is it creates a platform for businesses to communicate their message about their product or service in a 'long' format, in a longer message. So, instead of running short form advertising, 30-second commercials, or 60-second commercials, the advertiser is able to talk about their product or service for 30 **minutes** *or*

60 **minutes**. *Huge difference! The business owner can explain to the consumer who they are, what they are, and why to should use them. Also . . . this is hugely efficient in that the per-minute pricing is cheaper this way . . . versus buying individual commercials.*

JT: So, it's basically a radio show.

MW: Yes! It's a radio show...about YOU and your business.

JT: The big hidden gem is the fact that when people hear you on the radio, they automatically elevate you to celebrity status. When they hear you on your own talk show that puts you in a whole different light in their mind in terms of the credibility factor.

MW: Yes! The truth is ...that most people in the world are NOT on radio. So it automatically elevates you as the Expert and someone that the listener should pay attention to.

JT: So you essentially have 30 to 60 minutes to put your message out there. So, let's talk about the basics for a business owner, who has never done that before. So, let's start with timing. What does someone plan for? What's the ideal time for someone? 30 minutes? 60 minutes? Let's say you have someone in front of you who is saying, "Hey, I've never done block programming before...please guide me along. What do I do?"

MW: I always recommend 60 minutes. You're trying to attract people while they're in their car driving, running errands, and so forth. Let's say hypothetically they're going to drive their kids to a soccer game, or say they're going to a grocery store. They're going to get in their car at 3pm. They'll go and run to the grocery store and maybe they're going to be back in their car at 3:45. So, if you have a 60 minute show...the chances of the consumer/listener hearing about you is higher than if you only had a half hour show. So, if you have an hour's worth of time, you can talk to that person, reach that person, and connect with that person in their car listening to the radio from the beginning of the radio show and at the end of the radio show. Statistics show, and research shows, that you need to hear a message three or four times before you actually react. What happens in today's world, because we're so bombarded with messages...messages that are coming in different formats, whether it is on radio, on television, print, computer, your hand-held device. YOUR message needs to stand out. I believe a business will stand out with their own unique radio show.

Radio, to me is the best companion ever. Radio is a conduit to a listening audience of consumers. It's like a virtual neighborhood where consumers live.... and return to their favorite radio stations day in and day out. So when they tune on their favorite radio station, they hear about YOUR company. When you're listening to radio, hearing a message, in your car, by yourself listening to it, you are an extremely captive audience as a listener. As a consumer you are present and paying attention 100 percent.

Back to your original question, what would you recommend? I think they should contact me of course at Be Real Management & Marketing and I will put together a radio program. I determine what the unique selling is. Once we determine what is unique about them and why someone would use their product or service, then we build an entire show around it. It's really about me extracting from the business owner what they do, why they do it, and who their customer is. From that point, I will I create a radio show it in such a way it is attractive, compelling, persuasive, entertaining, informational.

One of the key things radio shows do for businesses is that they build trust. That's the biggest issue these days. Consumers don't know who to trust? With today's technology, businesses are growing so fast, and as a business owner if you have an opportunity to build and create trust with someone, you will never lose that customer.

JT: I listen to your show on the radio, and it's incredible how people equate credibility with hearing you on the radio. OK, I'm "Joe Business Owner" out there. I'm such a nervous person and I'm so shy I can't even begin to think about getting on the radio, let alone doing a radio show. What do we do with this person who is NOT a natural at getting on the mic?

MW: This isn't a problem. If a business owner is confident about their business and they are interested in expanding their voice to a bigger audience, whether locally, regionally, or even nationally, I would go to them, determine their unique selling proposition, learn what is unique about their business, and then I would hire a host. The business owner does not need to host their owner radio show....but could be the expert, in studio as the co-host or the featured on-air guest. When a business owner wants to expand his business using the radio show format, we can hire a radio host who knows exactly how to be on the radio. Kind of like you, Jim. Even though you're not a professional talk show host, you sound darn good. What the radio host will do is he will lead the show and the business owner on where we need to go. The message that needs to be communicated, including inviting listeners to call in during the radio program to ask questions. I'm producing it, I'm instructing on what the content needs to be, the show host is running the show and the business owner is the expert and will answer the questions that the radio host or call in listeners will ask. The show host will lead him through a series of questions: What do you do? What's unique about your business? Why should I call you, Mr. ABC Pool Company? The expert, the business owner doesn't even have to think of the answer because he already inherently KNOWS the answer! He already knows what is unique about his business, about his 'pool company', and why someone should call him. He might say things like, "Well, we use all natural products, we take pride in our service, we have licensed service people come out to service your pool, been in business for 35 years, or whatever it is you do as a pool company business. Answering questions is easy for the business owner. The show host will keep the show moving along maintaining listener interest, building trust, ultimately generating sales.

JT: I think this is a very important question for people, and where your expertise really comes in. People may blindly trust a sales rep for radio or television, "Oh yeah, do this, put your money here." I think it's very important where you run your blog programming, station, time, placement, etc. Talk about that. Where should someone's program be placed and how it will be most beneficial.

MW: Anyone who is reading this book, which I know a lot of you are, or are listening to their downloadable CD. First thing you do is call me! I have 15-plus years in the field creating successful radio shows and building company brands. There could be a checklist of items; let's go through a few of them right now.

Number One: Ask, "Who is your customer?" What is the largest demographic that buys your product or service? What is their age? Education? Sex? Married or Single? Homeowner? Etc.

Number Two: Then you determine what radio station best matches that demographic. You know basically what stations are in your city, so you have an idea what is airing. The radio station rep should be able to give you information that supports that demographic on any station that you call.

Number Three: Who else is running long-form (block programming) advertising on this station? Is there a competitor of yours on this station on the weekend? Typically these programs run on the weekend, so you want to know who else is running on the weekend.

Number Four: Pricing. Let's talk about this. You want to figure out how many minutes you're going to get for your long-form show. Let's say it's a 60 minute show, or perhaps it's a 40 minute show...what is it actually costing you per minute?

Number Five: You need to dedicate enough budget to run for a good period of time. Doesn't need to be huge, but whatever you decide, stick with it for at least three months. Preferably six months or longer.

Number Six: Be Consistent. Think of this as an investment. Think long term. What does the radio station contract commitment look like? Make sure to review terms before signing.

Number Seven: You have to make sure that a radio show is the right platform for your product or service. If you're selling hamburgers, maybe a radio show isn't the best for you. BUT, if you are teaching people and showing 100 different ways to cook a burger and webcasting the show and interviewing celebrity guests every week....then maybe it IS a good idea.

Number Eight: You need to have a compelling message. A strong call-to-action. What do you want the listener/consumer to do with the information they just heard about? Why should they act now?

Number Nine: Deliver on what you promise to the consumer. If you do, it is a home run. If you do not, the death of your company in the near future.

Number Ten: Stay the course

Those are the key things I would review with a business owner considering a long-form/block program radio show.

JT: OK, let's talk about pricing, and I know this is going to vary depending on where you are in the country and the station you choose. Can you give me a range someone would be looking at in terms of block programming?

MW: Yes....there are huge fluctuations in pricing due to the population and market size and if the city is considered a good radio market. If you're going to do block programming in San Francisco or New York, where there is mass transit systems there like BART or the subway, terrestrial radio is not in high demand. Typically radio is great for commuter cities where people are stuck in traffic in their cars. In San Francisco, people use mass transit systems or they walk. But, in places like Washington or Los Angeles, these are excellent radio advertising cities because of the large population size and the amount of traffic on the highways.

JT: Right, you are stuck in traffic listening to the radio.

MW: And in those cities, the big radio stations' pricing is commensurate to the size of the station and the size of their audience or market. If you look at Los Angeles compared to San Diego, or Inland Empire, the pricing will be lower in San Diego and Inland Empire due to smaller market size. Check around. Ask people, "Who are you listening to?" Most likely, the more popular stations will have higher pricing.

JT: Any range for half an hour?

MW: I just put together a deal for $300 for one hour in the Inland Empire area. In Los Angeles . . . for one hour, I have seen as much as $8,000 an hour. Let me tell you something, you get what you pay for. If you have a good show producer, someone who is putting together a good quality show with a good host and you're message is focused (and you have to be focused in your message) with a strong call to action, your radio show will be a home run. I've been doing radio for fifteen years and there is nothing that can give you that kind of a Return on Investment as Long Form Radio Advertising, regardless of a good or challenging economy.

JT: You can't discount the credibility factor. When people hear you on the radio, you are automatically the expert in their mind because you're on the radio. I think it is the best direct response vehicle out there. They hear on the radio, "Call now, pick up the phone. Go to our website. Register now." That's the point of marketing, direct response. Forget branding. You want direct response, which is exactly what long-form does for you.

MW: The key to long-form programming is to make it not sound like an infomercial, but to make it sound like part of a radio station programming, to sound like the rest of the radio station content. That's what really happens when you decide you want to create a radio show and become part of a radio station. You and your company becomes part of the line-up, you become part of that on-air radio team. You become part of the perceived value of a nationally syndicated talk show host. You automatically are an expert, you know more than your competition. Face it, most businesses are not on the radio. Yes, there are some, but not many. And, once you get on the radio, you need to stay on the radio because once you've started that course, you need to stay on that course. There are ebbs and flows in life and there are ebbs and flows in business and the economy. View this as an investment in your company today and for the future.

Wouldn't you want to be perceived as the best? As the Top Dog in your category? I believe that radio is the best vehicle. And if you can't afford the best station, then go to another station. Once you get on radio, you don't want to go off because whoever has been listening to your message, you want them to keep hearing your message.

JT: That's actually a million dollar tip. When you look at your business and then look at your competitors, most of them are not on the radio. By being on the radio, you automatically have elevated yourself above the completion. "Wow! He's on the radio!" I think people may not realize it until they actually do it, but the amount of people who buy from you, simply because they have heard you on the radio, and believe me, they've already determined that they're already going to buy from you, even though they don't know much about you or your product yet, but you are on the station. You must be real. The best. That's enormous.

MW: You can't really buy that.

JT: No you can't.

MW: Once you're part of the radio station line-up, you're part of the radio station on-air team, even if it is just on the weekend. When there is an event I guarantee, you will be mixing with and rubbing elbows with *those weekday talk show hosts and let me tell you something, they're going to say, "Hey! I know you." Because they listen to radio too. They're addicted to radio. They host shows during the week and they listen on the weekends too. They'll come up to you and say, "Hey, aren't you Jim Toner? You've been on for three years, five years, ten years?" You will be part of that radio network that elevates you above anyone else in the competition. You can't buy that. This is an amazing bi-product that will again serve to elevate you and your business above other...whether you are paying $300 per hour or $8,000 per hour.*

JT: Anything else in closing you want to ad?

MW: Radio works, people! Tap in to the radio stations' loyal listening audience with thousands of listeners waiting to hear about YOU! Build trust with that listener compelling him to buy from you. You can do a little, you can do a lot. You can air locally, or you can go national. You can air a long-form show, just like Jim Toner has done. He's taken a radio show, and with that same radio show, that good quality content and aired it in other markets. Now, you are not only monetizing yourself in your 'home' market, but with that one radio show, you're now multiplying that in other markets with exactly the same radio show. It's win-win. It's a home run.

JT: I like it!

And there you have some of the best information about radio advertising in the industry today. Get out there and use it.

Direct Mail

Aah, the lost art. Direct mail used to be the big thing before email came along. Guess what?

It is about to become the big thing again. Why?

Frankly, I think people miss their mail! These days people are so inundated with email that they never get good mail pieces.

It is a mistake to ignore the value of direct mail.

One of the things I like best about direct mail is the ability to directly track the results of its effectiveness, which is of supreme importance.

Especially if you are on a very tight marketing budget.

You also can tinker with and test your direct mail piece much easier than other types of advertising. Again, this can be done fairly inexpensively.

In keeping suit with all of our advertising formats, I **strongly** recommend that you know your target audience and where to find them.

I know that is kind of a given, but it is frightening how many business owners just use a scatter-gun approach when it comes to their advertising. The really cool thing about direct mail is that you **REALLY** target the people you want.

For this gold nugget, I interviewed Rich Selby of Selby Marketing Associates:

Interview with Rich Selby of Selby Marketing Associates and Jim Toner

JT: We are talking to Rich Selby of Selby Marketing Associates. Rich Selby has been in the fulfillment business for decades and is certainly an expert to say the least in many forms of marketing. But for the purpose of this interview I want to talk about Direct Mail. Direct mail is something that is a lost art, but I believe it also probably the "next big thing." Rich deals with the top marketers in the world, so when it comes to attracting customers with direct mail, I don't think there is anyone better to speak to. Rich, for those who may not be familiar, what is direct mail?

RS: Jim thanks for having me. As far as answering your questions about what is direct mail, its generating letters, postcards, any type of communication piece that goes out to a prospect or existing customer to keep your face in front of them so that they can never forget you. It is still one of the most cost effective mediums of soliciting business and increasing your business and maintaining your business relationships.

JT: Walks us through this. If someone decides they want to experiment with direct mail, where do they start?

RS: Let's start with what a customer needs first. Direct mail is only one component in the marketing program that someone should use. It should be supplemented with faxes, emails, mobile 2.40 marketing etc. When you make a commitment to do direct mail it needs to be part of an overall strategy that someone has and you need to be committed to doing a minimum of four mailing. The idea scenario is four to six according to what the industry analysis says. Next, your mailing will only be as good as your list that you provide so you need to really look at the profile of your customer and then if you are going to purchase a mailing list, you want to make sure it meets the criteria of your existing client base. These would be people who would purchase your product. So the first starting point is putting together your list and capturing your email address when you do a mailing so that you can stay in constant communications with them.

JT: Let me stop you there. This goes back to what we talked about when I was covering television and radio advertising. Direct mail is the exact same in as much as you have to know who your customer is. Even if you don't have any customers yet, you have to know who you are trying to attract. If you know who you are trying to go after, who is your demographic, we can find that person. So if your new, and don't *currently have any customers, you can go out and basically purchase a list of potential customers, thousands and thousands and thousands of names and addresses that will fit your ideal client profile*

RS: *That is correct, but it is really important to understand to deal with a quality broker because the ones that sell real inexpensive ones, let's say you buy a list with 10,000 people on it, if you have a 10%-15% drop off because of bad names, you haven't saved any money, so it is worth spending a few extra pennies to make sure you have a quality list.*

JT: *Let's touch on that. Where are the best sources for people to acquire quality lists?*

RS: *It depends on the industry that they are in. Different list brokers will actually specialize in specific industries. One place that we purchase our lists from is a company called Accudata. There are number of list brokers in the United States and through them, you can purchase a list that will give you a good return for the money you spend that you are going after.*

JT: *What can someone expect to pay for a quality list?*

RS: *It is based on how specific you want it to be. You can go right down to a person's income level, your gender, your level of education, where they live. The more criteria that you put in to hone down the list to real quality names, the more expensive it can be. Also, based on the industry you are going after, can determine what the list will cost.*

JT: *Is there a range that someone can be looking at?*

RS: *I can give you generalities.   It can be anywhere from $20 per thousand names to $1000 per thousand names. Then you get into how many times you are going to use the list. You probably want to do multiple mailings. When you select it as an option that you are going to mail more than one time, it will cost more as well.*

JT: *The more you use the list the higher the fee?*

RS: They will charge you either a onetime usage fee or a multi-use fee.

JT: To clarify, direct mail is exactly what it says, it's a mail piece. The reason I think this is so important is because everyone is always looking for the next big thing. A while back and actually still, E-mail marketing was considered, "the next big thing" I personally think this is going the way of the dinosaurs. I think people are so inundated with email that when they get a quality mail piece they are excited, like wow, I got something in the mail! Anytime you are looking for a customer or looking to grab someone's attention, if you don't get their eyes on it, it is worthless. I know I go through my email that I get, sometimes 100s a day that I don't even open. I delete, delete, delete, delete. I don't even read them. That doesn't help when you're trying to acquire a customer. But with a quality direct mail piece, you are half way there if can at least get them to look at it.

What are some of the strategies that you recommend for someone to make that happen? How do we make them look at it?

RS: One of the big mistakes I see people making is trying to get too much into the direct mail piece. So it ends up being an overload. All you want to do is hit a high point with your prospects to get them to either go to your website or to call into your company. The more you throw in there, the greater change that they are just going to toss it. We do sales letters, we do postcards. If you add personalization, which is the person's name, it increases the response rate by 29% is what the numbers show. It is important to understand what the motivational factors are when you are doing a mailing. One of the other things I see a lot of people making a mistake on is they will start off with, what is it going to cost me? Really, the thought process should be how much income can it generate for you, and how you can then build off of that. Remember, we want to get to that 4-6 pieces level which is when people really begin to buy.

JT: You brought up a very good point there as far as the cost. Because smart marketers and business owners know that what you should be looking at is not how much can I make on this person right now, but what is the lifetime value of a customer. So smart marketers will pay a lot of money for quality leads. Many business owners go into their marketing thinking, "I am kind of a shoestring (budget) so I've got to really save". That doesn't help you. You have to look at the lifetime value of that customer, should you acquire that customer. The idea is to get the customer at whatever cost and you work on the lifetime value. So you are saying the industry standards are showing about a four to six sequential mailing piece, correct?

RS: Yes. Let me back up a bit. Let me tell you a story of what happened today. A client that is in the financial industry calls me up and wants to do a mailing of 5,000 to 10,000 pieces, he has no idea if his postcard is going to draw or not. So, I suggested we look at what he has created as to his postcard and then we do a test mailing. This is extremely important because if you mail to 500 or 1,000 people and you get a 0% response rate or extremely low, then you know there is something wrong with your mail piece and you want to tweak it until you are getting at least 4%, and that would be on the low end. There are no guarantees, but we have had as high as over 18% response rate on some of the mailings we have done. We have had customers as well that have done 13 different postcards to see which pulls the best and the irony was they threw out the ones that were at the 4% spectrum, where most companies would kill for that kind of return.

JT: Yeah, the 2% is kind of the rule of thumb. 4% is killing it.

RS: A half of 1% to 1 ½% most corporations would say that was doing well, but in our world I don't know too many people that would be happy with that.

JT: Let's talk about the actual piece itself. Content is king. You can't just throw something out there and hope people look at it. You've got to get their attention. What do you find to be some of the most successful pieces? Is it postcards, it is a letter, is it a gimmick type of mailing?

Obviously it may depend on what industry someone is in or if you already have an established relationship with that person receiving the mailer or if you don't have a relationship with them. What are you finding to work best?

RS: *There are several approaches. You have your postcard, you have your sales' letter, you have your inserts with the sales' letter with some sort of a response mechanism and then you have another category, called lumpy mail, and lumpy mail refers to usually putting some sort of a gadget into the envelope or using some sort of vehicle so that someone is definitely going to open it. So case in point, we are going to start with lumping mail and work backwards. We've done mailings for example, one called the x-ray mailing and what happens is the message is actually printed on a piece of acetate with solid black and reversed out type so it actually looks like it is an x-ray. Then it is split into a grey envelope and then it is marked x-ray, do not bend. That has been a wildly successful promotion.*

Another one that we did a few years ago for a service company that was intentionally not taking ad space in the yellow pages at the time. We did a direct mail piece that basically said the phone company screwed up and left the ad out of the phone book. Please insert this before all the A's in your yellow pages. Their ad went into the yellow pages at a fraction of the cost and they were number one in the phone book and it pulled really well.

Another one we have been doing lately is a plastic garbage can. It's a small one and the sales letter is put inside the garbage can and the mailing label is put on the outside so it gets to the recipient and of course they are going to open it up to see what's inside. The letter starts off by saying, "I wanted to save you the trouble of throwing this letter out."

We do different from what most people are doing. We've done everything from aspirin to shredded money to bank back mailings and so on. The size of your list will dictate what makes the most sense.

We've had one customer that actually did a recording and we overnighted it to several prospects in a tape recorder. So, when the recipient got it, the Fed Ex box, and they opened it up, the tape recorder was there and they pulled it out and there was the message. That's an idea of lumping mail.

A sales letter is an extremely effective methodology of getting thoughts across. You really need to have a very good copywriter on it and it can range anywhere from 8-32 pages. Now some people will say, they are never going to read it, but it has a really good return on investment if it's done properly. That's the key. You have to spend money to do things the correct way if you want a good return.

There is another one where it looks like a hand written letter on yellow legal paper with blue lines. We print the message in a hand writing font and personalize it. It would say "Dear Jim" and the rest of the message. It is a one pager, really simple and that works incredibly well.

The last way is the post card. If it's a post card, you can personalize it, it can be generic. You can do what we call a pearl which is a personalized website URL so it would be WWW.marketing/JimToner or JT and you would put that in and when you go to the person's website, it populates with your name so it looks like it was created just for you. Basically anything that will attract your attention long enough to remember who you are. That's what the goal is.

JT: I hope the people reading this realize the monetary value in those last few paragraphs. I love that hand written note. Great idea. What everybody needs to understand is that there is enormous competition to get people's attention. Between the television, radio and internet, people are wired in 24/7. So you are battling for their attention which all goes back to why lumpy mail. Some people says that's silly lumpy mail, well if you get something in the mail that has a big lump in the middle of it chances are you are going to be interested enough to say what the heck is in there. You are going to open it up because if you can get them to put their eyes on it, it doesn't matter. What you said about the copywriting is probably even more important. The copy, and for those who don't know the copy is what the message is, and not everybody can write good copy. If you are not a very, very good copywriter or someone very good at getting a compelling message across, you need to hire someone to write your copy. And like you said Rich, 8 to 32 pages, for some people that might be well crazy, who's going to read it? It doesn't matter if they read it, what matters if they respond. Sometimes the headline alone is enough to get people to respond. I think it is crazy that all business owners do not make this an integral part of their business. I just think the competition being so tough in the other mediums, whether its television, radio etc., that direct mail is a phenomenal outlet.

RS: It has longer staying power than when you do TV or radio or even a billboard. Even if you happen to catch them at the right moment, most people can't remember it afterwards. We did something for a real estate agent which had the person's picture on the front in one reveal, and a house in the background and a for sale sign and then you tilted the card a little and it showed sold and the third reveal it showed the sold sign with the realtor and the house in the background. What we are trying to do is to create an impact. In that particular instance, people were so enamored with playing with it and seeing the different images that the retention was incredible that they never threw the card out. The bring it home first and let their kids play with it. That is the big advantage over a temporary impression you get with radio or television.

JT: Especially if you are doing sequential mailings. If nothing else someone might be thinking, "Who is this person sending me another piece of mail?" At some point they are going to look at it. If you have a compelling message, there is a good chance they will respond to it.

If you had an elevator speech for an existing business owner or a newly budding entrepreneur and you just had a quick elevator speech about direct mail marketing, what would it be?

RS: I would say to them, first of all direct mail is coming back. If you look at the real successful individuals, organizations and companies out there. The reason you see so much mail come from these people is because it is really working. As a side bar, I am working with someone who sells martial art videos and tennis videos and we are actually launching a piece tomorrow where it is geared towards tennis players. The first step in the sequence is the post card and then we are going to drive them to a landing page website and the next mailing that will be done is a tennis ball mailing where we bought used tennis balls and that would be part of the package that goes out to them. Anyone who doesn't use direct mail because they think it's too expensive or it doesn't work either hasn't worked with the right company or they don't know their true cost of client acquisition. In my opinion, there still is no more effective, affordable medium to get clients or prospects to respond, and become a client for you.

JT: I couldn't agree more. Thanks Rich.

CHAPTER 10

The Down and Dirty

O K gang, wake up call. I know we all want to believe it is a happy happy, joy joy world out there...but it ain't! As Rocky Balboa so eloquently said ...

It is a mean and nasty world out there

and it will beat you down if you let it.

We talked earlier about the supreme importance of customer service and how it really can make or break your business. Right now, I want to talk about what can happen no matter HOW GOOD, your service. There is a reason I call this chapter, The Down and Dirty.

The World Wide Web is a blessing and a curse. Personally, I am beginning to feel it is more of a curse. The web has given true weapons of mass destruction to some very evil and gutless people and organizations. Online defamation can happen to anyone with the consequences being devastating. Cyber bullying results in the deaths of God knows how many teens who commit suicide each year to cyber bullying.

Businesses are not immune. There are dozens of sites on the web where anyone can post an anonymous, false statement about you and your business that can literally put you out of business overnight.

There are many offenders to this crime. Many, operate under anonymity, while others, that are very well known, blatantly advertise what they do under the guise of "Consumer Protection"

My hope is that with the enormous damage this is causing to both businesses and individuals, laws will soon be passed to prevent this type of activity. But for now, it is out there, and it is dangerous.

I have brought in the best person I could think of to address this issue. He is known as the world's first, "Internet Bounty Hunter" Enjoy.

Interview with Michael Roberts from Rexxfield, LLC and Jim Toner

JT: I'm here with Michael Roberts from Rexxfield, LLC and this may be one of the most important chapters in the book due to the seriousness of it. Michael, I've seen your bio and what grabbed me was the statement that you are believed to be the world's first Internet Bounty Hunter. Is that similar to a reputation defender?

MR: That is part of my mandate. Companies specializing in online reputation management, they put Band-Aids on the wounds. My primary objective is to actually catch the people that are posting the diatribe. So people who hide behind the cloak of anonymity, my job is to drag them out into the full light of day with no identity being revealed.

JT: I want to really dig into this because again this book is for business owners and entrepreneurs. I hope they recognize the seriousness of this because literally businesses can be taken down overnight simply by some rouge posters online under the veil of anonymity putting whatever they want about an individual or a business without anything to back it up, they hide as they say under the anonymity and many of these posting make their way to the front page of Google. So, I want to start with that. What drew you to the industry and how did you get started because you've got a very impressive and interesting bio. How did you actually get into this industry, what drew it to you and what is it that makes you . . . I know a lot about you already and the background is beyond impressive, so let's start with what drew you to this and what got you started.

MR: Well, impressive is an interesting word. I'll swap it with anybody. In a nutshell, in 2004 I survived an attempted murder at the hands of my ex-wife and the judge didn't believe it. The county attorney didn't believe it. They pretty much thought I was the bad guy just trying to throw all types of charges at my ex-wife. Evidentially, over the next eight years was a battle for my children. She did get convicted of murder in the first degree and she is now serving a life sentence without the possibility of parole. In between the attempt on my life and her arrest, she had free reign to say whatever she wanted to say about me online, and she did. And that pretty much destroyed anything I had touched. So, any business relationship or job that I applied for, she was able to alienate me or estrange me from the people by the lies that she told. She did this anonymously and I would take it to the judge in the divorce court, for example, trying to get sanctions and also to show she is not a *healthy mother and the judge would simply say, "Well this is anonymous, prove it." Even though it was clear where it was coming from. In a previous life, I had a company called Mile 2 and we actually developed the first certified penetration testing exams and curriculum and we were literally training the U.S. Air Force Red Teams, before they were called Red Teams. These are the guys that hack enemy networks and keep hackers out of their networks. So we were training and certifying them and our business was on path to become a $20M or $30M dollar a year business, within two years, because of the service contracts we had, and yet my ex-wife, from a dial up modem in her mother's basement in rural Iowa, was able to destroy that business and force me to sell it for pennies on the dollar. Just to save the jobs, so she would leave the people alone, I was able to take some of my skills in IT security and adapt that to prove that she was the person responsible for these postings. It didn't actually get me anywhere, oddly enough, with the judge. He pretty much took the position that sticks and stones will break your bones Michael, get over it. And yet, I was being forced to pay $1500 a month in child support and couldn't get a job because I was vocationally a leper because of what my ex-wife was doing. As I started researching who else was out there, I realized there was a gap or there was a space that needed to be filled and I just naturally fell into that, under the brand Rexxfield. So, the first day I actually posted, "Hey this is what I do, I can find these people if anybody needs help, let me know." Within 48 hours I had a $30,000 contract with a $600M a year company who was having those problems and then there was no looking back.*

JT: So, in other words, there are a lot of companies out there that claim that they are reputation restoration companies or restoration repair or reputation protection companies, but you can literally take it to the next step and not only remove these posts, but you can actually find the perpetrator?

MR: Removing the post, we get that done along the way. I am going for the cancer. I want to cut out the sociopaths that are doing this to people and destroying their businesses and relationships and finances and everything else. If you can take them out, often the problem with stop because there will be sanctions against them or their victims will sue them successfully and so forth. But along the way, we have tools and we have people that are really good at burying or removing negative content from the Internet.

JT: What are some of the most heinous things you have seen? Because the one company we obviously want to talk about it is the infamous Ripoff Report but , what are some of the things you have seen just mom and pop businesses that have literally been destroyed by anonymous postings out there.

MR: There is a Ph.D. that I was doing some work for and she was actually suicidal. I knew she was losing it and I could feel her life slipping through my fingers. She was desperate for help because of the Ripoff Report. I actually called Maria Speth, one of the attorneys from the Ripoff Report. Some people think she is a silent partner. I explained the problem. I said I am not even charging this woman because she can't get a job. I'm not charging anything, it's a pro bono case, would they just remove it? I'm just worried that she will commit suicide. Her response to me was, "Michael this is the job for a medical professional, not social networking." It was just a bizarre response. The woman's life was literally in her hands and they just turned a blind eye.

Unfortunately, one client, actually a pair of concerned parents called me, their 21-year-old son likewise, his life was slipping through their fingers because he was being bullied as a result of a poor life choice that he made. He got drunk and he was persuaded to do something that he shouldn't do. It wasn't anything illegal, it was just morally questionable and this college newspaper blogged about it and it was on page one of Google, and he hung himself. We lost him. I was begging the university editor to pull it and this little kid, 18 years old, with all the power in the world, editing this little university newspaper took it on himself to say, "No, I'm protected by U.S. law, I can leave it there." Anyway, the kid's blood is on his hands.

JT: Absolutely horrifying story. But you said something there that I really want to touch on. You mentioned the word bullying. It is all over the news now, as it should be, it should be on the forefront, about the nightmares about bullying with children, but people need to understand that bullying is going on in the business world and if you are mom and pop business just trying to do your best out there when a competitor can get out there and anonymously slander your business and put you out of business. That is economic bullying. Not to mention the psychological factors involved in it but economically you are just destroying people and so you have gone out ... No go ahead.

MR: Well, the legal definition would be "tortious interference with prospective financial gain" and yes, it is cyber-bullying from a business perspective. So think about it: there are two electricians in a town, Pete Smith and Joe Brown. Joe Brown isn't good at what he does. He can't really get ahead and Mr. Smith is really, really good at what he does. So Mr. Brown spends a fortune on advertising but it's just like dog food, it doesn't matter how much money is spent on advertising on dog food if the dog doesn't like the taste, he's not going to buy it. The same thing applies to vendors of services that don't do a good job. So, rather than spending tens of thousands of dollars a year advertising in the local newspapers, he will all of a sudden anonymously post on Ripoff Report that Mr. Smith is a pedophile. Within a few days that will probably show up on page one of Google and all of a sudden the rumor mill starts, and he starts losing business. Where are they going to go? There is only

SEND IN THE WOLF • 189

one other electrician in town and so they move across to Mr. Brown because they don't want to even think about the idea of dealing with the individual against whom these allegations were leveled. So, Ripoff Report is really cheap marketing for unethical business people because it's reverse marketing. It's negative marking against their competitor.

JT: For the readers out there who may not be familiar, we are referencing a company called Ripoff Report. This is one... I've been a 25-year entrepreneur and I have been there, done that, and seen it all. This is one of the most frightening things I have ever seen. Simply because of how I guess ignorance might be the polite word the general public is regarding this site, Ripoff Report is often cited as the go to place to check out someone's reputation and when I say it is the go to place, my own attorney referenced it as something that people should check out. I have seen it on Fox News where people say; oh you can check a company out on Ripoff Report so it is supposedly, "The Place" if you want to find out if someone is legitimate. I'm going to let you explain a little bit more Michael, so everybody knows the facts about Ripoff Report and then I want to go into the relationship between Google and Ripoff Report and how this is literally destroying businesses.

MR: If it weren't for Section 230c of the Communications Decency Act, which was enacted in 1996 by the U.S. Congress and its wisdom, it would be extortion. But he is immune. Ed Magedson, the owner of Ripoff Report.com, is immune from any liability from anything that is published by a third party. So that could be Mr. Brown, the shady electrician posting on his website. So when Mr. Smith, the victim, wants to get that taken down. He can't even sue Ed Magedson for defamation because he is immune because of their sweeping immunity that has been granted even though it is probably being interpreted to be sweeping it. I have some theories how that can be challenged. But, because he doesn't have to remove it because of the immunity, he can actually say, "Well, *you can give me $5,000 a month Mr. Smith and I will cause it not to show up on Google." It is a classic shakedown. That is what it was called in recent filings by some lawyers in Florida. They actually described it as a classic shakedown with the exception that it has immunity through Section 230c.*

JT: Now, let me ask you because, that is what boggles my mind because for instance if someone is out at a bar drinking and God forbid they go out and they kill someone in a drunk driving accident. Oftentimes that bar owner is held liable. Now that bar owner did not drive the car and kill somebody by that bar owner provided the platform for it. So they could be held, so why can someone like Ed. Magedson skirt through this, and say well I didn't say it? He's providing the platform.

MR: Because of the law. The law literally gives sweeping immunity for everything except racketeering laws. Now, funny enough, if it was somebody else saying that I will remove it, the person that posted it, I will remove it from Ripoff Report if you pay me money, that would be racketeering. But if Ed Magedson says it, it's not because he has immunity.

JT: Isn't it also correct that they actually won't remove it. They will just put up there that Ripoff Report that they have investigated it and approve it, but it still stays there.

MR: Yes, but there has been examples recently brought to my attention where it disappears off of Google and whether it be meta tags that they put into the pages, to index, I'm not sure. I don't actually care; I just want to catch the bad guys. I've given up researching what Ripoff Report does. I just want to shut them down and my mission is to see its owner in jail. I believe, I now know he is actually involved in a case against me and I will be filing charges. I have actually filed complaints because he knows I am coming after him and so it in his best interest to destroy my reputation and discredit my research. He has actually trying to help get my ex-wife out of prison to torment me at the thought of losing my children to her again. It's not going to happen, of course, but it is not stopping him from doing what he is doing. He actually engaged a guy to spread all sorts of rumors about me from pedophilia to wife beating to tax cheating. You name it; it is called a kitchen sink attack. It's all been thrown at me.

JT: Also, I didn't really delve in your background that much, but you are also a licensed private investigator, a journalist, so you are well aware of these type of attacks and what is happening, but hopefully the readers understand that why the reason I wanted Michael to say these things, these attacks coming against him, is because again this is the pre-emanate source that people are told to go to, Ripoff Report. Well, here is the owner of Ripoff Report and here is what they are resorting to, to try to destroy someone. If you are a small business owner out there and a competitor decides to get you, that is what is coming. Now, here is the other side of the coin, that again boggles my mind, I didn't get it until you explained it a few weeks back when we spoke, but the rankings of Ripoff Report on Google. Because everybody out there, if you want to be shocked, go out there and Google your name and you might be a little shocked to what you see. But, oftentimes if you are in business especially what you might see on the front page of Google is Ripoff Report. Now, explain to the folks how Ripoff Report ranks so high in Google and, what, if anything can be done about that.

MR: Well, I have a theory on that. It is a working theory. I've done some very crude and empirical testing which supports my theory. Google will call it, the reason they put Ripoff Report out there is they want diverse results. They don't want someone with lots of money make sure any good stuff shows up on page one by doing lots of search engine *optimization. They make sure there is something negative in there. Google doesn't care; once again they are immune because of the same law as Ripoff Report Section 230c. The reason I think Google wants negative stuff on page one is for this: if I do a search for Pete Smith Electrician, Des Moines, Iowa, I've just told Google I am looking for an electrician. I'm looking for an electrician in Des Moines, Iowa and I'm specifically looking for Pete Smith, the electrician. I've given Google a lot of information in the five words I have just entered. That is a lot of intelligence, its actionable by Google. They now have my attention because I'm using their search engine. They need to monetize the search that I am doing. If they serve out the results with Pete Smith electrician.com in position one, which is what they will probably do and rightly so because it is the appropriate result that I am looking for and I click on his home page, Google just lost control of me and I'm on Pete Smith's website. That is not good for Google's business. They need to make money out of me, somehow and I believe they deliberately elevate negative stuff to page one to repulse me from the real Pete Smith, whether it is true or not and then chose an alternative click rather than his website. And, of course, on the right hand side of the Google search results there is probably 5-6 electricians who are all paying Google ad words for every click they get on those ads. So by turning me off Pete Smith, instead if I click on Andy White, electrician on the right hand side, Google will make $2-$3 from that click-thru. That money was made at the expense of Pete Smith because Ripoff Report is not true in most instances in my experiences.*

JT: So, in other words they are making money from Google ad words intentionally by letting the negative information rise to the top.

MR: That is my hypothesis and Google.....

JT: It sounds pretty clear to me. That is a very good hypothesis.

MR: You have to look at the cross-sectional diagnosis, there are other factors and Google's defense is that they want diverse results for the reason that I explained before. It doesn't cut it for me. I've done the research. I've created 30 blogs once, well, 15 different blogs with two different examples, each pair of blogs were identical except for some modifying key words. For example, it might have been Angela Barnes is a wonderful babysitter. I highly recommend her to all my friends. Then a few other paragraphs. Then I copied and pasted the content and changed the modifiers to Angela Barnes is an atrocious babysitter. I would never recommend her to my friends. Identical prose and text except for the adjectives. Well, all of these got launched at the same time and over the following weeks I did some pretty crude monitoring of the search results without clicking on any of them to see what happens and guess which ones on about 87% of the time showed up above the other ones? The negative ones.

JT: One of the biggest problems the public has is they often have their heads buried and they don't want to believe that companies would do things. I literally watched a sixty minute interview with one of the founders of Google, Sergey Brin, and he was directly asked about negative information on the front page of Google and it hurting people and his answer literally was that there is nothing they can do to control that.

MR: He's a liar. I can say he is a liar.

JT: It was such a blatant lie, because to me, who knows nothing about computers or algorithms or code, I know nothing about this, but what I do know is his company creates that. So you are telling me you created it but there is nothing you can do about it? To me it was a blatant lie. That just does to show what you call a theory, I don't think of it as a theory at all, I think that is the answer. Google gets paid by letting negative information flow to the top so they get their Google ad words. This is what is destroying businesses. That's what I think. So, again for the folks reading this, this is not a conspiracy theory, this is real stuff happening and real business owners are being put out of business by negativity out there. Ok, it's out there. We know it's there. What can be done to prevent it or get rid of it? How can someone protect themselves? People reading this right now are scared to death; "OMG" my competitor is going to put some bad things about me. What can be done? How can people take action about protecting or again getting rid of these things?

MR: Unfortunately, they have to take Google's advice. Google's response when you complain about this stuff is normally, "Get out there and create some positive content." That in my view, it is just junk. That is just spam. If you don't need it out there, why create it? Well, Google wants more content to index because that gives them more platforms to put their advertising on, unfortunately that is what they need to do until this law is changed. They need to create a buffer around their name, a buffer around their reputation. Positive and mutual content that will hopefully dilute some of the garbage because if they don't take a proactive approach and build that fire breaker around their name, somebody is going to do it for them and it is not going to be pretty.

JT: So, in other words, get out there and start creating a lot of content, maybe get some blogs going, some things about whatever your business is. Anybody. It doesn't matter what your business is. There is a lot of content you could create that buffer but don't just let your name sit out there.

MR: And don't copy and paste, copy and paste, because Google has what's called duplicate content filters and if it sees multiple version of exactly the same text, it will only index one of them and the other ones get penalized. So you need to actually be creative and change things.

JT: Let's say someone, it's too late, they haven't built their firewall and they are in trouble now and there are some things out there that are hurting their business and they are looking for someone who can correct this. You hear a lot of ads on the radio, people, companies advertising, we will take care of your reputation. We will fix it. But, you are different. I want you to quickly tell the story because it related, it hit with me because my home state is PA and you related a story to me the other day about the governor of PA. Can you let the readers know what that was? I want people to understand how good you are at what you do.

MR: Sure. Oh thank you. Tom Corbett used to be the attorney general and he had two critics on Twitter, one of them name was Casa Blanca PA and the other one was Bfbarbie. They are very critical of him and he wanted to know who it was so, it was my understanding that he convened a grand jury to get a subpoena issued to Twitter, but Twitter didn't like that and went public with it and it ended up in a big uproar and got egg on his face. I was really surprised that he got the governorship actually, the election. I had heard rumors he hired five lawyers, state lawyers and $100,000 in taxpayer's money might have been spent on this. I really don't know if it was rumors but it was a great effort. They got nowhere. They never identified these people and I was curious about that. I was reading about that while I was on hold with a software company support call and in the seven to eight minutes I was, after I decided I'd have a poker round, I was able to identify one of the antagonist, not by name, but by location. Their mother tongue is not English. It was a very rare language and I was able to build a profile for that person that would have been very, very easy for the governor's office or the attorney general's office at a time to finish them off. That took *seventeen minutes as opposed to a grand jury subpoena that was rejected anyway.*

JT: 17 minutes. That's amazing. Now, you are one of what two people in the world that do what you do, is that correct?

MR: No, I'm sure there are more people that could do it but just do other things with their gifts. But as far as actually offers the services I've trained a total of three or four people. Two of them kind of messed things up. They're trying to do it on their own now, but being such a small niche of what we do, I've had to several cases come to me because the problems got worse with the people I had to let go and I do have one guy who is still on my team that is very, very good. So between us, we have done a lot of work for civil as well as criminal law enforcement agencies. We've been able to crack some cold cases for them that were going nowhere.

JT: You work with large corporations and small businesses, correct?

MR: We've done work for heads of state and their families, government, Fortune 100 companies, right down to teenage kids that are getting bullied.

JT: Wow. So a business owner can reach out to you and say Michael here is what I have going on and you will be able to at least decipher what is happening and potentially eliminating the problem depending on how bad it is?

MR: Hopefully. I don't take on any cases that I don't think there is a high probability of success and by setting those standards we are approaching 90% success rate because we do say no to quite a few cases.

JT: Are there any particular timelines for having things corrected? I know every case would be different depending on how bad it may be but are there average timelines where people can see positive results appear about them and the negative results disappear?

MR: Once again, we can arrange that. My passion is catching the bad guys and that can be as quickly as seven to eight minutes as we discussed and there are cases that are still opened. We have not been able to solve it yet. But as far as making a difference, if it is Ripoff Report, it is very, very difficult; it will probably always be on page 1. So, we have developed a new method to deal with that. It's a website called AuthorizedStatement.org. We spent a lot of time and money persuading Google that it is an important website and even though Ripoff Report may not get buried, or removed without a court order, we can often give a victim a very, very loud voice above or very close to the Ripoff Report posting where they can respond to the post and tell their side of the story which they don't want to do on Ripoff Report with a response there because it makes Google go crazy and elevate it even further. You do not want to respond on these gripe sites. The more chatter there is on the page, the higher it will rank.

JT: Also, that is true for all the other gripes I assume? There are a lot of these sites out there, complaints board and all these things that people can get on so they are all the same? The more people actually look at those complaints, the higher they get ranked.

MR: Particularly if it is updated with responses and arguments for the victim and the accuser. The best thing is to just let sleeping dogs lie.

JT: But you guys can actually find who these people are that made these posts and things can be taken from there?

MR: In most instances, yes. Sometimes we can do it completely in the shadows. Everything we do is legal and admissible in court. We don't hack, we don't break the law. Sometimes though, if we fail, what we call social engineering and social forensic efforts, we may have to resort to a court subpoena if the victim has the financial and emotional wherewithal to take it to court. The court, for us, is always plan B. We try to get it sorted out before they do any filings.

JT: I would imagine if someone made an anonymous post and they were confronted that they were caught, I would imagine they would be quite frightened and they would want to go away and not cause any more problems.

MR: We had a great one the other day. It was once again back in the New England area. There was a website set up, an actual custom website, Pete Smith, Electrician Suck.com, that type of thing. The client engaged us. They didn't want to make a lot of noise. They wanted to find out who it was quietly. We discovered there was another ten websites that this person had also set up anonymously using disposable credit cards with Go Daddy and hiding behind proxies, in fake I.D.s and so forth. Within a week we were able to physically trace this person to a Dunkin Donuts, free Wi-Fi. Not only did we catch him in the act and positively identified the individual, we were even able to get the surveillance footage of him sitting at the keyboard at the Dunkin Donut store doing what he was doing. We initiated communications with this individual with some screen shots of that video footage and surprise, within about eighty minutes all ten websites were removed.

JT: Wow. That is absolutely incredible. Again, I hope people reading this, especially business owners understand how this equates to dollars and sense, not only money that you would lose that if after you have a customer, but money you are losing because you don't even get the customer because they are researching you and they are seeing all these bad things. If you are in a business itself that sells big-ticket items that can be a lot of money that can really put you out of business before you even know what hit you.

MR: Yeah.

MR: There is no way of quantifying the damage with this type of thing. It is kind of like in the reverse sense, if you have an armed guard at the bank, you don't know how many robberies were thwarted because of the person's presence. Conversely, you don't know how much business you are missing out on because of the people who might have called you, but read this garbage instead.

JT: I've experienced it first-hand. One of my companies is a real estate investment training firm and we have had this happen to us. We have had competitors post negative things about us. All anonymous, of course. We've had people outright tell us, well I saw this on, X site so I can't do business with you. It is just, it is what it is. Thankfully there is someone like you now that is providing a platform for some justice and for people to fight back and get some justice. If people want to reach you, I imagine you are available for hire?

MR: Like I said, we are pretty selective in the cases we take on. I want to make it very clear, we don't need... if someone is being victimized like this, and we don't need your money. We've got plenty of work. We are not going to take on a case unless we think we can get somewhere with it. They can go to our website which is Rexxfield.com. We are at their service.

JT: You will be able to, if it is a case that you either don't have time to take on or want to take on, can you refer them somewhere else or are *there other people that can help with these things? I know there are a lot of people who advertise these things. The question is who can do it, and who can't.*

MR: Once again, there is stuff that's advertised as reputation management. We do have people that do it. I will often refer that business on to trusted third parties. And they are not the big names that you see on the radio advertisements. These are small boutique outfits that are really good at what they do. And I do want to say that this business is as much a ministry for me as it is a business. So about 80% of the work we have done has been pro bono. I'm not going to be doing any more of that this year because we took on way too much pro bono and it is very difficult to feed the family when you are overwhelmed with free cases. There are no strings attached. We are good at what we do. We are expensive, but we are not going to gouge anybody and we will be honest with you, with your problems. If you go to our website, submit your contact details and then you will directed to what is called a case intake interview. It is a form that asks a whole bunch of questions about your particular case. Within five minutes I will have a pretty good idea if we can help you or if you need somebody else and we can refer you on.

JT: I just want to bring one more thing up. I'm glad you said it. I think this will help clarify for a lot of folks. There is a difference, there is a reputation management companies and these people will monitor what you are doing out there and provide content for you. But then what you do is you will come in once someone is attacked. Is that correct?

MR: Yes. We clean up.

JT: You are the cleanup guys?

MR: We are the cancer surgeons. The cancers are the sociopaths that wielded their poisoned pen diatribe behind the cloak of anonymity.

JT: I love it. You are the best. That's it. It is Michael Roberts, Rexxfield founder. Check them out at Rexxfield.com. Lots of great stuff on their website. Truly a very good education. A really eye opening education.

MR: With two XXs.

JT: Yes. Rexxfield.com. Thank you Michael.

MR: My pleasure.

So there you have it; the harsh reality of the World Wide Web.

The best way to defend against online attacks is by making sure you have happy customers.

If you are attacked by an anonymous poster online, you do have some recourse. Should you discover what you feel to be an outright false attack against you, my recommendation would be to contact Michael Roberts of Rexxfield and have the person tracked down.

You do have legal recourse should the accusations be proven false.

I suggest you use them.

CHAPTER 11

Now What?

In the words of the immortal Jim Morrison of the Doors, "This is the end, my only friend, the end." Well not really . . . I'm just a big music fan and felt the need to put musical references in this book.

So there you go.

Now what?

Well, whether you know it or not, if you have read this book closely, you have received a million dollar education. How do I know that? Because it cost me that much to know what I wrote here, that's why.

The question that remains is what will you do with the information?

Here let me help you along.

If you are currently a business owner, budding business owner, or entrepreneur . . . you'd **BEST** heed everything I wrote in these pages. Now that's a pretty good jumpstart. You don't need to figure anything out at all. All you need to do is what I told you to do.

What's that you say?

You need a bit more handholding? Not feeling that confident or maybe you are looking to make a quantum leap in your business income?

If the above sentences apply to you and/or your business...it's time to call:

The Wolf

One of the biggest problems many business owners / entrepreneurs face is that they spend far too much time in their own heads and can't see the forest for the trees.

I cannot only see the forest; I can tear it down and rebuild it to suit you.

If you're thinking, "Oh boy, here comes the sales pitch," you would be partially correct. Yes, my services are for hire, but only on a very limited basis . . . for the **RIGHT** businesses and entrepreneurs.

I am fortunate to have been able to build multiple thriving businesses that provide me with a very comfortable income. I do not **NEED** to do anything business wise that I do not want to do.

On the other hand, I do **VERY** much enjoy working with the right individuals and businesses in getting them on track, out of trouble, and or doubling their income, freedom and security.

I will tell you freely that my services do not come cheap, but I am known as the **WOLF** for a reason.

I get results...

Period.

Below are just a few of the subjects that you will either find yourself in deep water with at some point, *or* should be seriously considering adding to your business for a quantum leap in terms of cash flow and net worth:

- **Business Consulting**

- **Marketing**

- **Employee Issues**

- **Legal**

- **Real Estate Investment Consulting**

- **Real Estate Investment Portfolio Building**

- **Fitness**

- **Personal Development**

- **Charity Endeavors**

- **Seminar Creation**

- **Product Development**

- **Book Creation**

- **High End Mastermind Group**

- **And many more...**

Can you guess the one thing that all of the above have in common?
MONEY!

Either loss of or acquisition of. One of the two will happen. Here is a hint . . . *TAKE THE MONEY!*

Not sure yet?

Here are a few testimonials that may help you make a decision:

"Jim Toner is a living super hero!"

-FIVE TIME BEST-SELLING AUTHOR AND REAL ESTATE LEGEND, FRANK MCKINNEY

"Award Winning"

-PERSONAL REAL ESTATE INVESTOR MAGAZINE

"An entrepreneur that may be the stake in the heart of the recession."

-PITTSBURGH BUSINESS TIMES

Are you ready to get serious about your business?
Go to www.CreatingWealth101.com.

Special Message to Anyone Contemplating Starting a Business

Good for you . . . smart move.

Maybe.

Although much of the content in this book may frighten away fledgling business owners, the flip side of the coin is the financial windfall that can come with being your own boss.

We are not only in the greatest time in history to jump into entrepreneurship, but many Americans are actually doing it. Tens of thousands of baby boomers, dissatisfied with just existing, are deciding to dive into their own ventures.

As I said, that is great.

However . . . you will most likely get just one shot. Do **not** go blindly into the arena. Smart money surrounds themselves with smart people. For those who do not, that vast majority will fail. Over 50% of new business owners fail in the first few years and over 80% after five years.

How would you like to stack the deck in your favor? I suggest we have a little chat to not only be sure you know what you are getting into, but how you can also have ME as the guy who has your back.

That, my friends, is money *very* well spent.

CHAPTER 12

Final Word of Warning

I don't want to burst anyone's bubble, but it's a dirty world out there. You would think that after all these years I would have long since stopped being surprised by what I see happening in the business world.

But I am not.

Not all things are as they may seem and not all people you deal with are well intentioned. On the contrary, many things you see, especially with the internet, are nothing more than smoke and mirrors.

Those so-called *experts* and *gurus* are nothing more than second rate con men hiding behind a website and slick marketing.

To be fair, I am not just talking about making money, self-improvement, business gurus etc. I am talking about every level of business and the government as well.

Let's start with the internet.

As I said in an earlier chapter, the internet can be a blessing and or a curse.

The curse comes in when it becomes the be all and end all for "definitive" information on a given subject. People see something online and they believe it as gospel truth.

One of the world's biggest online *consumer protection* websites where people can go to find out if someone is *reputable* is nothing more than an extortion website. See the interview with Michael Roberts.

The Better Business Bureau (BBB) is another *trust worthy* organization people hang their hat on. DO you know you can "buy" a good rating? Shocked? Most people think that the BBB is an organization that provides a public service to protect the public.

Nope.

The BBB is a FOR PROFIT business. Rumor has it that HAMAS, yes the terrorist group, has an A + rating with the BBB.

No joke.

How many times have we seen public figures revered for what they *supposedly* have accomplished, only to find out it was all lies?

The great P.T. Barnum once said, "Never underestimate the ignorance of the general public." He was dead on.

However, let me take it a step further.

I call it **WILLFUL** ignorance.

The gut instinct that we all have that is a warning signal for us is all too often ignored. The bad guys know how to make that happen.

In the seminar world, they employ loud music and fast talking speakers **TELLING** you that you are going to be a big success as

long as and only if you work with them. They employ tactics designed to control you and how you think thus making you an easy
mark for what they have in store for you.

They call it sales, I call it bullshit.

I'm not saying that every consultant, guru, politician out there
is bad or out to harm you. What I am saying is that **most** fall far
short of being able to help you. Their combination of skill and
ethics is in short supply.

If someone has got the goods, oftentimes they are secretly waiting to prey on the unsuspecting sheep. If someone means well and
really wants to provide you with a good product or service, they,
too, fall far short on being able to deliver.

In the real estate investment world of which I have been a part
of for twenty-five years now, it is almost laughable in how many
new *gurus* and *experts* are out there. Most of them, and I mean
MOST of them are not even real estate investors nor have they
done more than a handful of deals.

Slick marketing and big advertising budgets make up for the
shortfall in skill. Can you say, President of the United States?
Yup.

Here are just a few of the industries I have personally witnessed
intentional fraud and corruption:

- Investment Real Estate
- Health Care
- Seminar Industry
- Government
- *Any* of the so-called expert industries

- Sports world
- Consulting Businesses
- Local and National Law enforcement
- Construction Industry
- Marketing

I could go on, by why bother. I think you get the point. It's kind of like a sharp stick in the eye right?

So is it all bad? No, it's not. There are lots of very valuable people in every industry who can not only help you but also do it the right way. The trick is to find them.

Here are a few tips on how to do that:

1. Believe almost **NOTHING** you read online. In case you did not know, most is either planted and/or created in order to intentionally mislead or fulfill an agenda.

2. Believe almost **NOTHING** you see in the media, unless it can be substantiated.

3. Do not be overly persuaded by any type of "Voted Best" types of labels. They can be and *are* purchased.

4. Put a lot of stock in what is being said about said person and or company by **LEGITMATE** industry leaders. They will not risk their rep to say something good about someone who is not.

5. Find out what the majority of customers say. Don't look for 100% approval because it doesn't exist. Every now and then a customer gets a bug up their ass and decides to take revenge on the Internet.

6. ***TRUST YOUR GUT.*** This is a very big one that people ignore.

All I am saying is this, be careful out there.

If it seems I have a chip on my shoulder, I do. I don't like fakes, frauds and phonies. Especially when they look for and prey on hard-working folks who are just trying to make their life a little better.

So the million-dollar question is:

Who's afraid if the Big Bad Wolf?

Answer . . . anyone who does not want to be exposed for being incompetent, dirty, and a fraud.

For those looking to make life better, make more money, and have more fun and live a life that matters . . . I'm on your side.

I'm the Wolf . . .

And I'm a good person to know . . .

ABOUT JIM TONER

Jim Toner has enjoyed a long career as a real estate investor, radio show host, speaker, and consultant.

He has spoken throughout the country on the value of intelligent real estate investing and has appeared with the likes of Frank McKinney, Bill Bartmann, Sharon Lechter, The Napoleon Hill Foundation, and many more.

Jim's expertise in making real estate investment "user friendly" for the general public has put his services in very big demand. People routinely pay $2,000 to $15,000 and travel from all over the country to attend his real estate investment programs.

Jim, an accomplished entrepreneur who has been in the trenches of the real estate investment world for over twenty-five years, has taught thousands the path towards financial freedom by using his custom *12 Little Houses Plan.*

He is an active philanthropist having been nationally recognized for his work with veterans and the homeless. He is an active member of Frank and Nilsa McKinney's Caring House Project

Foundation as well on the Advisory Board Chair of a Pittsburgh, Pennsylvania Salvation Army branch.

He currently works with a limited Private Client Group as well as coaching groups, both of which have waiting lists. He occasionally accepts new private coaching clients on investment real estate and entrepreneurial / business issues.

For information regarding Jim's programs, speaking engagements, or availability for consulting, contact Natalie at theexecutivetalk1@gmail.com.

Recommended Reading

Many people have asked, "Jim, how did you do all this?" For me it all started when I picked up Napoleon Hill's book, *Think and Grow Rich.* Reading that book changed my world.

Charlie "TREMENDOUS" Jones said, "You will be the same person five years from now as you are today except for the books you read and the people you meet."

I made a decision to be a different person. My recommended reading list is constantly expanding.

Here are a few books that I would recommend be a part of anyone's library.

Albom, Mitch – *Tuesdays with Morrie: An Old Man, a Young Man and Life's Greatest Lessons, The Five People You Meet in Heaven*

Bartmann, Bill – *Billionaire Secrets to Success, Bouncing Back*

Brady, Shelly – *Ten Things I Learned from Bill Porter*

Brown, Les – *It's Not Over Until You Win*

Camp, Jim – *Start with NO*

Canfield, Jack – *Dare to Win*

Clason, George S. – *The Richest Man in Babylon*

Collins, Jim – *Good to Great*

Cousins, Norman – *Anatomy of an Illness*

Dennis, Felix – *How to Get Rich*

Eker, T. Harv – *Secrets of the Millionaire Mind*

Harnish, Verne – *Mastering the Rockefeller Habits*

Gitomer, Jeffrey – *The Sales Bible*

Haggai, John E. – *Paul J. Meyer and the Art of Giving*

Hill, Napoleon – *Think and Grow Rich, Positive Action Plan*

Hoffer, Eric – *The True Believer*

Jones, Charlie – *Life is Tremendous*

Keith, Kent M. – *Anyway: The Paradoxical Commandments*

Kennedy, Dan – *No B.S. Marketing to the Affluent, No B.S. Ruthless Management of People and Profits, No B.S. Direct Marketing, No B.S. Wealth Attraction for Entrepreneurs, No B.S. Sales Success, No B.S. Time Management for Entrepreneurs*

Kroc, Ray – *Grinding It Out: The Making of McDonalds*

Kushner, Harold S. – *Living a Life that Matters*

Landrum, Gene N. – *Profiles of Power and Success, The Superman Syndrome*

Lechter, Sharon – *Three Feet from Gold: Turn Your Obstacles into Opportunities*

Mandino, Og – *The Greatest Salesman in the World, A Better Way to Live, The Greatest Miracle in the World, The Greatest Secret in the World, Og Mandino's University of Success*

McKinney, Frank – *Burst This!, The Tap, Dead Fred, Flying Lunchboxes, The Good Luck Circle, and Make It Big*

Mother Teresa – *A Simple Path*

Olson, Jeff – *The Slight Edge*

Peters, Thomas J. – *In Search of Excellence*

Peters, Tom – *Re-Imagine!*

Philips, Bill – *Body for Life*

Proctor, Bob – *It's Not About the Money*

Robert, Cavett – *Success with People*

Rohn, Jim – *The Seasons of Life*

Stovall, Jim – *The Ultimate Gift*

Wilde, Stuart – *The Trick to Money is Having Some*

Wooden, John – *The Essential Wooden*

Recommended Charity

Caring House Project Foundation.

For more information, go to:

www.Frank-McKinney.com

Notes

www.ingramcontent.com/pod-product-compliance
Lightning Source LLC
Chambersburg PA
CBHW060546200326
41521CB00007B/501